D0913428

the warren

a roleplaying game
by **Marshall Miller**

*"All the world will be your enemy,
Prince of a Thousand Enemies.
And when they catch you, they will
kill you. But first they must catch you;
digger, listener, runner, Prince
with the swift warning. Be cunning,
and full of tricks, and your people
will never be destroyed."*

Richard Adams, Watership Down

BULLY PULPIT GAMES

#TheWarrenRPG

The Warren and *Abingdon Meadow*
© 2015 Marshall Miller

Artwork, layout, and *Bayou Dupre*
© 2015 Bully Pulpit Games LLC

ISBN 978-0-9883909-4-2 (Paperback)
ISBN 978-0-9883909-5-9 (Hardback)

Second Printing March 2016

apocalypse-world.com

Marshall Miller
Writing and Design

Jason Morningstar and Steve Segedy
Production, Development, and Additional Writing

Karen Twelves
Editing

Rachel Kahn and Tony Dowler
Art

Brennen Reece
Layout and Visual Design

We'd love to hear about your experiences with *The Warren*!
You can reach us and find out about our other games at
www.bullypulpitgames.com

Thanks

Designer's Thanks

Jason Morningstar, Steve Segedy, Meguey Baker, Vincent Baker, Avery Mcdaldno, Jonathan Walton, Sage LaTorra, Rich Rogers, Tim Franzke, Stras Acimovic, Christopher Stone-Bush, Filamena Young, F. Dudley Staples, Brandy Cunningham, and Liam and Adeline Cunningham-Miller.

Additional Thanks to B. Dennis Sustare, Brennen Reece, Rachel Kahn, Claudia Cangini, Tony Dowler, Karen Twelves, John Sheldon, Tim Rodriguez, Renee Knipe, Kristin Firth, Eric Mersmann, Marissa Kelly, Whitney Beltrain, Ajit George, Adam Drew, John Stavropoulos, Carrie Ulrich, and the many Kickstarter backers who helped make *The Warren* a reality.

Playtesters

Stras Acimovic, Mikael Andersson, Meguey Baker, Victoria Baker, Stuart Chaplin, Joel Coldren, Jesse Coombs, Jason Cordova, Stephen Crawford, Jim Crocker, Jamey Crook, Jeffrey Davis, Alison Davis, Lauren Demaree, Steven desJardins, Alex Dodge, Clinton N. Dreisbach, Jaye Foster, Jeremiah Frye, Ethan Gibney, Bret Gillan, Michael Godesky, Matt Gwinn, Dave Heeney, Joe Hill, Kat Hill, Justin Hirt, Monika Hortnagl, Greg Jansen, Rob Karachok, Aine Keefer, Robert Keefer, Stephen King, Carley Knight, Renee Knipe, Rob Laman, Daniel Lewis, Monte Lin, John Marron, Tom McGrenery, Anna McKibben, Andrew Medeiros, Jason Morningstar, Scott Morningstar, Sean Nittner, Ian Oakes, Ray Otus, Kevin Petker, David Poole, Hank Raab, Ferrell Riley, Jesus Rodriguez, Noam Rosen, Timothy Schneider, Steve Segedy, Derek Smyk, Melissa Spangenberg, Kelly Vanda, Parrish Warren, Victor Wyatt, David Zumora, and our friends at Games on Demand events everywhere.

Acknowledgements

The Warren is based on the groundbreaking games *Apocalypse World*, by D. Vincent Baker, *Bunnies & Burrows*, by B. Dennis Sustare and Scott Robinson, as well as the classic novels *Watership Down*, by Richard Adams, and *Fifteen Rabbits*, by Felix Salten.

Sage LaTorra and Adam Koebel's *Dungeon World* and Avery McDaldno's *Simple World* were also indispensable in the design and development of this game.

Apocalypse World
apocalypse-world.com

Dungeon World
dungeon-world.com

Simple World
buriedwithoutceremony.com / simple-world

Fifteen Rabbits
books.simonandschuster.com / Fifteen-Rabbits

Watership Down
books.simonandschuster.com / Watership-Down

The *X-Card*, developed by John Stavropoulos and repeated here with permission, is an excellent tool for creating a safer gaming environment to explore the beauty and terror of nature.

There is another book entitled *The Warren*, by Fred L. Tate. While it is also a book of rabbit fiction, it is wholly separate from the present text.

If you would like to read more about rabbits, both real world and fictional, there is a mediography in the back (see page 110).

Contents

Foreword

Mankind has always told stories about animals, possibly even before language. Imagine cavemen getting excited over the drawings of megafauna in the caves of Altamira, Lascaux, and Arnhem Land, perhaps acting out the motions of throwing spears with atlatls while shouting and jumping. Every culture has stories of animals, with the animals described ranging from the very natural to highly anthropomorphic or even the avatars of gods. So when you sit around a table making up animal stories, you are connected to all cultures now and in the past.

Many of the folktales are explanations about nature or the animals themselves. The names of the stories give away what the tale is about. *How the Zebra Got its Stripes*. *Why Opossum's Tail is Bare*. *How the Buffalo Came to Be*. Other stories are fables to give guidance or provide a moral. A huge number of these are rightly or wrongly attributed to Aesop, a slave and storyteller of ancient Greece. *The Ass and the Pig*. *The Crow and the Pitcher*. *The Dog and Its Reflection*. *The Fox and the Grapes*. And, of course, *The Tortoise and the Hare*. Some of these fables are found as a similar story in different cultures, such as the variants of the *Frog and the Scorpion*, *The Scorpion and the Turtle*, *The Farmer and the Viper*, and others in which someone assisting another gets paid back foully ("But why? It's just my nature.").

One of the most popular types of animal stories is that of the Trickster, an animal that succeeds because of its cleverness, instead of size, claws, or fangs. In the southwest of North America, the animal is Coyote; on the northwest coast, it is Raven; in western Africa, it is Anansi, the Spider. But every culture has tricksters, though not all of them take animal form, often being some type of spirit or demon. In many of the stories, there seem to be blends of spirit and animal, such as the kitsune foxes and tanuki raccoon-dogs of Japan, the Monkey King of China, and Cagn of the Bushmen, who can shape shift into any animal, though most often appears as a praying mantis.

The Trickster is a most appropriate model for stories about rabbits (as you will generate during play of *The Warren*), since nearly every animal a rabbit encounters is bigger, stronger, and fiercer, and many of them would be happy to eat the rabbit. Br'er Rabbit (from the Uncle Remus tales) and El-ahrairah (from *Watership Down*) are archetypical trickster rabbits; if you have not read those stories, stop now and go find them. Even Loki and Odysseus may have something to learn from trickster rabbits.

But when playing a rabbit game, do not feel bound by a particular style or model. There is no reason for your rabbit not to be a fearless hero, charging to attack a threatening fox, or a maternal doe striving to impart caution and wisdom to her kits, or an aging rabbit longing to creep into the garden for one last taste of strawberries. *The Warren* allows you to add your storytelling to a wonderful and long tradition.

Just as people (and animals) have different personalities, so, too, do storytellers come in all forms. Whatever story you choose to tell through your rabbit will be the right story, especially if the other players all enjoy the process and share in the adventures. As Richard Adams said, "Everyone's good depends on everyone's cooperation," and the same is true in game-playing. Have fun as you play *The Warren* and contribute to the world's library of animal stories.

B. Dennis Sustare
Designer of Bunnies & Burrows

Jumping Off

The Warren is a tabletop roleplaying game about a community of rabbits and their struggle to survive.

If You've Never Played a Roleplaying Game

Players in *The Warren* get together with friends and explore the lives of rabbits by narrating their adventures and rolling some dice. The game is mostly conversation, so if you're happy to talk about adventurous rabbits with your friends, you're already most of the way there.

If You've Played Other Roleplaying Games

In *The Warren*, players create characters, a community in peril, and play to find out what happens to them. *The Warren* features rabbit characters, rules that are mostly about the fiction rather than numbers, and a format that is equally suitable for one-shots and campaign play.

If You've Played Other Games that are Powered by the Apocalypse

You'll feel right at home in *The Warren*—your instincts won't lead you astray. Some features to keep an eye out for are claiming Player moves from a shared pool, birth and death as a part of play, and player-driven move creation.

Down the Rabbit Hole

The Warren is a game about intelligent rabbits trying to make the best of a world filled with hazards, predators, and, worst of all, other rabbits. While the rabbits in your games will solve some of their problems and learn some new tricks along the way, they are still bound by their anatomy and place at the bottom of the food chain.

The Warren is primarily a game about survival and community. There are many creatures, humans included, that are bigger, stronger, meaner, or more numerous than rabbits. The seasons and the elements do not care that rabbits are only little things. Rabbits cannot hope to meet these threats head on. Only through speed, wits, and keeping a cool head can rabbits hope to avoid the dangers of the world outside their warren.

Warrens are systems of interconnected tunnels and dens dug to shelter a community of rabbits, and they face dangers as well. Inequity, scarcity, and contempt seed dissent within rabbit society, just as they do human society, and ideological differences can destroy a warren as surely as any human machine. The rabbits in your game must decide for themselves what it means to be a rabbit and how to repair and sustain their warren so that it can thrive.

In the Warren

Warrens start and end at any one of many entrances to the surface and include the many bolt-holes that surround a warren's perimeter. Underground, rabbits build straightaways or runs that connect the fur-lined burrows where they sleep and birth their young. They also dig out around roots and stones, burrow drops to lower tunnels, and create stops where they can hunker down, exposing their flanks to protect their head when a predator confronts them in their home.

In hard-packed soil or clay, warrens are small and compact but in loose, sandy soil, warrens sprawl for hundreds of meters. Typical warrens of two to twenty rabbits can be relatively innocuous, often intentionally so, but where rabbit populations explode, their digging has been known to erode hillsides and undermine buildings.

Preparing to Play

The Warren can be played in a single 2-hour session or over multiple sessions. To play *The Warren*, you'll first need to gather two to four friends (three to five people total).

Most of you will be playing specific rabbits but you should pick one player to be the game master, or GM for short. People who play rabbits will largely control their own, individual rabbit— their thoughts, their actions, their fate. This rabbit is their player character, or PC.

The GM, on the other hand, will largely control the rabbits' surroundings—the land and weather, the non-player character (NPC) animals and humans, and the consequences of PCs' actions. The GM, at least, should be familiar with the rules of the game but all players will benefit from having read them.

Print out a copy of the rabbit playbook for everyone at the table. Print out a GM reference sheet and a World playset (if you plan to use one) for the GM. Make sure everyone has something to write with and a pair of six-sided dice (2d6). Some index cards, tokens, and scratch paper can also come in handy.

The rabbit playbook, GM reference sheet, and a variety of setting materials can be found on the Bully Pulpit website at *www.bullypulpitgames.com/games/the-warren.*

Ways of Playing

Gameplay in *The Warren* is broken up into units of play called chapters. Each chapter focuses on a specific set of PCs, their fates, and their contributions to the living history of the warren. Some PCs will survive and others will not but all will leave their mark.

The game is designed to play well in a single chapter, to fill a single evening or a slot at a gaming convention. It can also accommodate a series of linked chapters that form a campaign. Depending on how many hours you play, you might even play through more than one chapter in a single session.

Subsequent chapters will continue the warren's story. Some PCs will carry over to the new chapter but others will be new, replacing PCs who were retired during the last chapter or to allow a player to make a new character.

The chapter format is well-suited to intergenerational play, with some or all of the players choosing to play the last chapter's offspring and immigrants as PCs for the new chapter.

The end of a chapter (or session) is also a good time for a different player to take on the role of game master, giving the previous GM a chance to play a rabbit of their own.

Setting, Theme, and Tone

Before the game starts, take a moment to discuss the type of session you'd like to have. Are there specific settings or themes that you'd like to explore during play? What type of tone are you looking for? These questions are best presented for general discussion with the goal of reaching a consensus.

Rabbits live everywhere that humans do. Where we go, rabbits go—to the New World, to Australia, to hundreds of islands, to outer space. The default setting questions in this book suggest the British countryside, while one of the included World playsets is set in the bayou country of Louisiana. Your warren could be in a wild place like a South African river basin, the Canadian tundra, or the tropical forests of Laos.

Human spaces make a great backdrop for your warren as well, helping players imagine the world around the warren and the challenges it might face. So your warren could also be under a bush in Hyde Park, on the grounds of a Buddhist temple, or even on the White House lawn.

Don't forget that your setting isn't just a place but also a time! How would the invasion of Normandy, a Minoan harvest festival, or the colonization of Hawaii shape the fates of rabbits?

The rabbits in *The Warren* are an abstraction, a reflection of how we as humans think and behave and also a reflection of how we view rabbits. Across many human cultures, rabbits have come to symbolize woman and children, sexuality and innocence, empire and oppression, witchcraft and magic, monsters and prey, fear and friendship, travelers and tricksters. There's even something kind of kitschy about rabbits. Consider how these themes might factor into your games.

At the table, *The Warren* can also adopt a variety of tones—do you want romping adventure or biting satire? Are you looking for a desperate drama or something out of folklore? Discussing tone beforehand helps get everyone on the same page so they can work together to achieve that tone. This is also a good time to talk about elements you'd be excited to experience during play, as well as things to intentionally avoid.

See Establishing the Tone (page 66) for more on this, as well as details about how to run a very apocalyptic game using Dark Mode!

Anthropomorphism

Anthropomorphism is an important aspect of all animal stories. To what extent will the animals in question be portrayed as they exist in the wild or as representations of humans? Wildlife documentaries represent one end of the spectrum. Animals are filmed exactly as they exist in the real world and any sense of story derives from careful editing and voice-over narration. On the other end of the spectrum are stories where animals talk, dress, behave, and live like humans—walking upright, wearing clothes, drinking tea, dueling with pistols, and driving sports cars. In between these two extremes lies a fertile middle ground, and the ways in which animal characters do and do not adhere to their real world counterparts are critical details in any animal story's setting.

The animals portrayed in *The Warren* are part of that middle ground, though they are decidedly more like their real world counterparts than like humans. To an outside observer, animals in *The Warren* largely appear as they would in our world, but within each species is a very human social environment.

In *The Warren*, animals are self-aware, capable of rational thought, and enjoy rich emotional and intellectual lives. Animals also speak to one another as humans do. Like many groups of humans, animals in this world are primarily concerned with the members of their own species and do not go out of their way to converse with members of other species. Finally, animals in *The Warren* are considerably less constrained than their real-world counterparts with regard to their social organization, falling into many of the same ideological traps that human groups do. Rabbits in *The Warren* need not adhere to the strict social hierarchies that exist in real-world rabbit warrens—they are free to live and love as they see fit.

"Actually, real rabbits..."

During play, it may be tempting to bring up the finer details of rabbitry, like "the way rabbits really behave," "how fast rabbits can really run," or "how much a rabbit really eats." In truth, even a lagomorphologist (a scientist who study rabbits) would have a hard time answering these questions without numerous qualifiers—every species of rabbit is different and rabbits behave differently in the home than they do in a laboratory or the wild.

Instead, focus on the commonalities among rabbits. What you think about the rabbits in your game is more important than what "real" rabbits do.

Playing the Game

From the first moment you sit down to play *The Warren*, the game is a conversation. Players will first spend some time together creating a group of rabbits to play during the game and the types of rabbits each person wants to portray. One player will act as the GM and ask some questions of the other players—their answers will flesh out the PCs' warren and the problems that it faces, to be further developed in gameplay.

The Conversation

Playing *The Warren* involves the GM and all the players engaging in a conversation. The players will describe their characters' words, thoughts, and actions. Meanwhile, the GM will describe the world surrounding the PCs, its inhabitants, and the consequences of their actions.

When players describe doing something that is a given, the GM will describe their success. When players describe their PCs doing something that is impossible, the GM will tell them so and describe their failure. The imagined events that everyone is contributing to, throughout the conversation, is known as the fiction.

Everybody will ask and answer questions, and these contributions will change the details of the fiction. There is no fixed order to who gets to talk when, just the normal flow of a regular conversation— sometimes you'll be talking, lots of times you'll be listening, and once in a while someone will politely interrupt. At times, even the rules will politely interrupt the conversation in the form of moves.

Moves

Moves are the core mechanism of *The Warren*. Moves work by advancing the fiction. There are two broad categories of moves— Player moves and GM moves.

Player Moves

Player moves all represent important aspects of being a rabbit. They are broken into three categories: Basic moves, Special moves, and Character moves.

Basic moves are things that all rabbits do frequently in their day-to-day lives, while Special moves are important things that rabbits do, though perhaps less frequently. Character moves are things that make a rabbit unique, a special trait or aptitude that only they possess.

Not every action a PC takes will correspond to a move. Much of the time you will just describe what your rabbit does, says, or thinks and the GM will likewise say what happens.

Triggers

The text of each Player move begins with a trigger, a concrete event in the fiction, which always causes the move to take effect. Sometimes a move's effect involves a die roll but not always.

Whenever a player takes an action that triggers a move, the conversation pauses while the move is resolved, and then the conversation continues, taking into account the effects of the move. Everyone at the table should keep an eye out for situations where a move might be triggered.

If it is ever unclear whether a move has been triggered or not, then the GM should ask additional questions to clarify the situation. Sometimes this will mean asking the player what they are trying to do and discussing ways that they can make the fiction match the move that they want to trigger. Other times players will describe both their action and its outcome and you may have to backtrack to where their action should trigger a move. At times, players may even describe taking an action that triggers a move and then realize that they don't want to make that move and need to describe a different course of action.

Player characters may only trigger moves that are available to them—Basic moves, Special moves, and Character moves. They cannot trigger moves chosen by other players or moves that have been crossed off due to scars (see page 45 for more details). Characters won't necessarily trigger all of the moves available to them during the course of play—it's entirely up to the actions they take in the fiction.

Rolling the Dice

When a move calls for a roll, it will usually be presented as "roll+" followed by a PC stat, e.g. roll+Swift (see page 28 for more on Character stats).

Unless otherwise stated, this means that the player who triggered the move should roll two six-sided dice (2d6) and add (or subtract) the value of the listed stat from their sum. The move will then list the possible outcomes according to the resulting sum.

Frequently, a low roll will elicit a move by the GM, which is detailed on the next page. The GM will never need to roll the dice.

Forward, Ongoing, and Hold

Some moves will use words like "forward," "ongoing," or "hold." These are bonuses that you can use in play.

When a move tells you to "take [some number] forward," e.g. take +1 forward, that means you get to add that number to your next roll. Sometimes it will specify which type of roll you can apply the modifier to.

When a move tells you to "take [some number] ongoing," e.g. take +1 ongoing, that means you get to add that number to each roll thereafter. Sometimes a move will specify which rolls the ongoing modifier will apply to or a condition under which the ongoing modifier no longer applies.

When a move tells you to "hold" some number, e.g. hold 2, that means that you have already succeeded and you may activate the move's effects that number of times when you see fit. It might be immediately, it might be a little later in the conversation—it's up to you.

GM Moves

GMs have their own moves. Just like Player moves, GM moves help move the fiction forward. Unlike players, GMs will never need to roll the dice. GM moves work a little differently and are more direct—often prompting the GM to introduce a specific type of complication or adversity to the story.

GM moves are either "soft" or "hard." Soft moves introduce a threat or complication—something that the PCs can respond to, overcome, or avoid. Hard moves, on the other hand, introduce the hardship or consequence itself. Most of what a GM says while playing *The Warren* can be considered a move of one sort or the other.

Soft moves are important because they telegraph what might happen in the fiction, giving players an opportunity to act and change or avoid that outcome. Soft moves are changes to the fiction that often prompt players to make a move.

Hard moves are the inevitable consequences that result from soft moves or unsuccessful Player moves, and they often involve mechanical penalties. Using a hard move without a preceding soft move will feel especially harsh to players.

Threat and predator moves are GM moves that are specific to certain aspects of the fiction.

For more on GM moves, see page 56 in Running the Game.

All fiction is about people, unless it's about rabbits pretending to be people. It's all essentially characters in action, which means characters moving through time and changes taking place, and that's what we call "the plot."

Margaret Atwood

Playing a Rabbit

In *The Warren*, you start the game with a single player character, a rabbit, through which you interact with the fiction. Throughout the game, you may end up playing other rabbits.

As a player, your agenda is to play your character like a real "person." This means imbuing them with their own opinions, agendas, hopes, strengths, and foibles. This means they are aware that their actions have consequences, for themselves and others.

All rabbits start play as members of the same warren. Your rabbits might not start out or end up as the best of friends but they will often rely on one another to survive.

A Note on Character Conflict

Sometimes players' characters will come into conflict. This is all fine and well. Sometimes rabbits will be just horrible to one another. This too is fine. It is important, however, that character conflict should not spill over into player conflict. If you think things might get deliciously ugly, it's a good idea to check in with the other player to collaborate on the dark path ahead.

Creating Characters

Before play begins, each player must create a rabbit character to play. Players should create their characters together, at the table, rather than in advance of a game. There are five steps to creating a player character. As you complete each step of character creation, mark your choices on your rabbit playbook and let the other players know what you are marking on the sheet.

Character Creation

1. Choose a Character move for your rabbit
2. Assign stats to your rabbit
3. Determine your rabbit's Panic level
4. Select your rabbit's looks
5. Pick a name for your rabbit

Character Moves

The first step in creating a PC is choosing a Character move (see page 94). Players should claim their characters' moves one at a time, starting with the person newest to roleplaying. Character moves are moves that only your rabbit can make, so no two PCs should ever have the same move. Even if you gain additional Character moves later on, you cannot take moves that another PC currently possesses. Choose carefully because your first Character move will be one of your rabbit's most defining features.

Stats

Stats represent qualities that are vital for rabbits' survival, and will be used when making moves. Rabbits are, to a greater or lesser degree, Strong, Swift, Shrewd, and Steady.

Strong rabbits are better at fighting off predators and digging.

Swift rabbits have the best chances of escaping threats.

Shrewd rabbits are better at assessing situations and communicating information.

Steady rabbits are less likely to panic in dangerous situations and more likely to birth bigger litters.

No rabbit will be adept at all of these. When creating your PC, assign one modifier to each stat. The modifiers are +2, +1, +0, and -1. Some Character moves will even allow you to increase your stats; however, stats can never go above +3.

Panic

Rabbits exist at the very bottom of the food chain. To survive, rabbits must constantly be alert to danger and behave conservatively to avoid putting themselves at risk. When rabbits take risks or are directly threatened, they must struggle to keep it together and risk panicking. Panic often spells doom for a rabbit.

In *The Warren*, each PC has a Panic score, which gauges how close that character is to panicking. Crossing an open area, entering a hostile warren, getting caught in a snare, standing up to a more important or dangerous rabbit, or interacting with a predator might all constitute taking risks or being threatened and cause that character's Panic level to increase. Rabbits that are injured or are birthing a litter are particularly vulnerable to panic.

A rabbit's Panic level starts at zero—they are totally calm. As things get complicated, Player and GM moves will cause that Panic level to rise. When a rabbit reaches its maximum Panic level, it panics and things get ugly.

Each rabbit's maximum Panic score starts at 5 and is modified, up or down, by their Steady stat (e.g. if Thistle's Steady stat is +1 then Thistle's maximum Panic is 5 + 1 = 6). For more information about what happens when a rabbit panics, see Panicking on page 43.

Looks

Although the rabbits in *The Warren* may all be of the same species, no two will look exactly the same. Choose a look that matches your vision, perhaps corresponding to your rabbit's name or personality.

BODY
Lean, Stocky, Compact, Long, Frail, Sick, Runt

COAT
Lush, Sleek, Distinctive Markings, Unusual Color, Mangy, Singed

EARS
Long, Short, Floppy, Tattered, ID-Tagged, Just the One

PARTS
Buck, Doe (Pregnant)

Some Facts About Rabbits

- Rabbits are herbivores that live on six continents.

- Rabbits are active in the daytime (diurnal), at dawn/dusk (crepuscular) or at night (nocturnal) depending on predation.

- Rabbits weigh 1-4 lbs and can run up to 18mph.

- Rabbits have 28 teeth that never stop growing, two rows of incisors but no canines.

- Rabbits are born blind and nude; they open their eyes at two weeks, are weaned at one month and are ready to reproduce at three months.

- Does average five litters of 1-12 kits per year but often have as many as eight litters.

- Rabbits experience 80% mortality by three months and 95% mortality by one year—50% of adult rabbits will die in a given year.

Names

The last step in creating a rabbit is to choose a proper name for it. Good rabbit names come from nature. Consider names based on grains, herbs, flowers, trees, weather, or features of a pastoral landscape.

Some excellent rabbit names include:

Barley, Lily, Honey, Holly, Pumpkin, Thorn, Dusty, Midnight, Patches, Poppy, Snow, Pine, Floppy, Basil, Misty, Nutmeg, Breeze, Dewdrop, Charcoal, Sandy, Truffle, Olive, Ash, Chestnut, Ivy, Meadow, Jack, Parsley, Foxglove, Cutter, Lightning, Rose, Gale, Dandelion, Tin, Willow, Straw, Cotton, Thyme, Wind, Sunshine, Rainstorm, Peanut, Swiftpaw, Windrunner, Sundancer, Nibble, Digger, Squeak, Moonhunter, Raincatcher, Blackberry, Coriander.

Writing your PC's name and "buck" or "doe" on a folded index card is a great way to help other players remember who's who.

Putting It All Together

Once you've created your rabbit, you are ready to play. Don't think too hard about your PC before play starts; instead, let their personality, situation, and history come into focus during play. Let their choices and the details added to the fiction during their first chapter shape them.

The lifetime of a rabbit lasts seven years—
eight years at most. And while it is beautiful,
it is also full of terror and flight...
Be happy that you are alive, my children!

Felix Salten, Fifteen Rabbits

Player Moves

During play, PCs will have a variety of moves available to them. There are three types of Player moves: Basic moves, Special moves, and Character moves. The Basic and Special moves are detailed here. Character moves are listed in Appendix 1 (page 94).

Basic Moves

Basic moves are central to rabbits' day-to-day lives and are available to all PCs.

⊞ RESIST PANIC

When you expose yourself to new dangers, roll+Steady. On a 10+, you're unshaken. On a 7-9, you manage to keep it together but take +1 Panic. On a miss, take +1 Panic as you cower, hesitate, or flee—the GM can offer you a worse outcome, a hard bargain, or an ugly choice.

The GM may tell you that your action requires that you must resist panicking when you are exposed. That could mean crossing an open area, standing up to an authority figure, becoming trapped, or any other situation where threats might exist. If your roll succeeds, you've accomplished the action. If you exceed your maximum Panic, bad things happen. See Panicking on page 43.

⊞ SPEAK PLAINLY

When you reason with another animal, roll+Shrewd. On a 10+, NPCs will do as you ask given the proper assurances. On a 7-9, they do as you ask provided you meet one of their demands now.

Speaking Plainly is all about getting others to go along with your ideas. It's not a move you use directly on the other PCs, it's one you use on individual NPCs or even whole groups of NPCs. Your words may only Help/Hinder other PCs or cause the two of you to Compete.

⊞ PAY ATTENTION

When you give your full attention, roll+Shrewd. On a 10+, hold 2. On a 7-9, hold 1. On a 6-, hold 1 but you open yourself up to danger. Holds may be spent, 1 for 1, to name a sense and ask the GM one of the questions below. The GM will tell you what your sense reveals; take +1 forward when acting on the answers.

- What here is the greatest danger to me?
- What will happen if I stay very still?
- Where can I flee to?
- Are they telling the truth?
- What do they wish I'd do?
- How could I get _____?

Giving your full attention is the way you discover additional details about a location, an NPC, or a situation after the GM has told you what you're generally experiencing.

⊞ BOLT

When you make a run for it, roll+Swift. On a 10+, you run like the wind. On a 7-9, you run fast enough but choose one:

- You don't end up exactly where you intended.
- It takes more out of you than you would have thought; take -1 forward.
- It's much closer than you care for; take +1 Panic.

Bolting is a rabbit's first instinct and primary means of avoiding danger. Bolt can be used for short bursts of speed but, in a pinch, it can also be used when covering longer distances over land, such as attempting to reach a distant warren.

Their defence consisted of watchfulness,
their resistance was the quickly awakened
sense of fear that shot through them;
and flight, their artful, dodging flight,
to which they took in an instant,
was their way of fighting.

Fifteen Rabbits, Felix Salten

SNEAK

When you take pains to avoid notice, roll+Shrewd. On a 10+, pick three. On a 7-9, pick one:

- Behind cover
- Silent
- Downwind
- No tracks

Going unnoticed is the best way to avoid becoming a predator's next meal or avoid having to explain yourself.

HELP/HINDER

When you help or hinder another player character's rabbit, roll and add whichever stat the GM deems appropriate. On a 10+, give +1 or -1 to that player's roll or Panic. On a 7-9, do the same, but your fate is tied to theirs.

Helping and hindering are your primary ways to act on other PCs. The Help/Hinder move usually requires that your PC be present when another PC makes a move and that you say or do something to them that would reasonably make it easier or harder for them to accomplish their goal.

You can also use your words and actions to embolden them or cast doubt upon them by modifying their Panic level. This can be especially important when it comes time to Birth a Litter or when rabbits are close to Panic.

By committing to share their fate, you are not necessarily sharing the same fictional fate; however, you might suffer a hard move from the GM if the person you are helping or hindering rolls a 6-, take Panic or a modifier on a 7-9, or suffer some similar but independent fate, depending on the move in question.

Special Moves

Special moves are also moves that all PCs can make. Like Basic moves, they are central to rabbits' existence; however, these are moves that PCs will only occasionally make.

⊞ RELAX

When you play, groom, or rest in relative safety, subtract 1 from your Panic.

Occasionally rabbits will find time to rest and recover, time to enjoy the wonder of nature and joy of companionship. Be it hours or days, Relax is always marked by the passage of time. A safe, quiet space can be a comfort when preparing to Birth a Litter.

⊞ STRUGGLE

When you struggle to free yourself, roll+Strong. You may then take Panic, 1 for 1, to increase your roll. On a 10+, you manage to wriggle free. On a 7-9, you can wriggle free if you are willing to take a scar. On a 6-, you can't escape and you take a scar anyway.

Occasionally rabbits will become trapped, pinned, or snatched up by a predator. This move offers a chance to escape if you are desperate enough.

All beaded with dew
dawn grass runway
Open-eyed rabbits hang
dangle, loose feet in tall grass
From alder snares.

Gary Snyder, Myths and Texts

⊞ COMPETE

When you compete with another PC rabbit, both of you choose a value on a die and then reveal it. If one rabbit's die shows a higher face, they get their way and choose a value from one of the dice—both of you take that much Panic. If neither is higher, no one gets their way and you both take Panic equal to the dice value.

When similar situations arise between a PC and an NPC, always fall back to the question: What do you do? By describing your character's actions, you enable the GM to determine their consequences, be they obvious success or failure, a GM move or triggering a player move. See Fighting on page 44 for more on this.

Competing with other rabbits is stressful, even for the victor, and when competition gets heated, you can't rely on the victor to win graciously. Competition can take many forms but it always comes down to who comes out on top or who gets their way.

When you Compete, others may still Help/Hinder either rabbit.

Some Facts About Rabbits

- Largest rabbit: 50lbs, 4'3", and insured for $1.6M.
- Highest jump: 3.28ft.
- Longest jump: 9.84ft.
- Biggest litter: 24/26 survived.
- Oldest: 18.88y.
- Longest ears: 31in.
- Most ears: 4.

⊞ DIG

When you dig in the earth, roll+Strong. On a 10+, you scratch out a simple burrow or otherwise quickly shift some dirt. On a 7-9, choose one:

- You can only dig enough space to squeeze yourself into.
- Your excavation is unstable and temporary at best.
- You take significantly longer than expected.

Rabbits build warrens as permanent places of safety as well as smaller burrows as temporary shelters. In the real world, female rabbits do much of the excavation in preparation for birthing litters, but in *The Warren*, rabbits are free to divide the labor as they see fit. When you dig, it's also a good time to make a map of the resulting tunnels and/or add them to a larger map of the area surrounding the warren.

⊞ MATE

When you mate with another rabbit, take +1 ongoing to Help/Hinder that rabbit until you mate with someone else. If you are different genders, both of you hide zero or one die in your fist. On the count of three, open your hands—two dice means the doe is pregnant and she may give birth whenever it feels right.

Mating is a crucial part of rabbit life and any rabbits may mate. Mating intensifies rabbits' relationships and provides insight into each other's disposition. Mating can also result in pregnancy. In the wild, rabbits can birth many litters over the course of their lives but if being pregnant slowed them down, there wouldn't be nearly so many rabbits today. Of course, every litter is different— the experience of pregnancy and its aftermath is largely up to that rabbit's player.

If anyone at the table has reservations about including this or any other move in your game, consider removing it entirely (see below) or introducing the X-Card at the beginning of the game (see page 109).

Playing Without Mating

If you wish to exclude the Mate move from the game or want to explore these other equally important relationships, consider replacing Mate with Best Friend and Littermate. These may also be useful moves if you want to play *The Warren* with children. Players should feel free to incorporate these moves into the game but may not take advantage of more than one of these relationships concurrently.

▦ BEST FRIEND

When you have a best friend, tell them so and take +1 ongoing to Help/Hinder that rabbit until you decide to be best friends with someone else.

▦ LITTERMATE

When you are born to the same litter, share your earliest memories and take +1 ongoing to Help/Hinder that rabbit until another relationship becomes more important.

⊞ BIRTH A LITTER

When you birth a litter, roll and subtract your current Panic to determine the number of kits that are born. On a 10+, it's an unusually sizable litter—increase your Panic to maximum. On a 7-9, a normal-sized litter is by no means easy—take +2 Panic. On a 6-, it's all just too much and few if any survive. The GM still gets to make a hard move but this is a good time to check in and make sure other players are comfortable with the fiction.

Other PCs can Help/Hinder a doe, modifying her roll or Panic to achieve a desired outcome.

Birthing litters is one outcome of mating and important for the health and growth of a warren. A doe may Birth a Litter when the time feels right—the process takes about 15 minutes in the fiction. Of course, sometimes the best times are precisely the worst times!

When the birth is finished, name the kits. They are hairless and fragile now but by the next chapter, they will be out on their own.

If you know you don't want to play out the actual birthing at the table, trigger it at the end of the chapter—you'll still birth some new rabbits but it can all happen off-screen, between chapters.

⊞ INNOVATE

When you do something unheard of, imagine what your actions would look like as a move. Say what triggers the move and roll. On a 7+, work with the GM to write the move—it is now a Special move for the remainder of the game and your roll stands. On a miss, it's not something rabbits can ever do and there will certainly be consequences.

Intelligent creatures will often discover new behaviors or capabilities that were, theretofore, unheard of. When creating a new move, write a trigger that characters can initiate by taking decisive action (e.g. "when you do a thing," not "when you try to do a thing") and write the move's results from the perspective of that character rather than saying what an NPC or part of the world does (e.g. "you suffer a thing," not "they do a thing to you").

Move triggers are like wishes—the wording matters! The more narrowly you specify the trigger for your innovated move, the less likely you are to duplicate Character moves, which should be avoided, or to encounter other unintended effects later on.

Most innovated moves will involve rolling and adding a stat and will follow the success (10+), success but... (7-9), failure (6-) structure; however, they don't have to—don't be afraid to get creative and use other move structures if it fits the setting and fiction!

Innovate is a powerful move, to be used intentionally. It can be used to allow rabbits to manipulate objects or adopt new behaviors. It could also be used to permanently change the setting by introducing supernatural, mythical, or spiritual elements. It could even be used to adjust the degree of anthropomorphism on which the game is centered. Use it wisely, probably after some discussion with the other players.

⊞ TIME GOES BY

When months or seasons pass, roll the dice. As a group, decide which die represents births and which represents deaths. Add rabbits to the warren according to the birth die and subtract rabbits from the warren according to the death die.

This move is especially useful when you want to play a game of *The Warren* with children or when players do not wish to incorporate the Mate and Birth a Litter moves into the game. It allows the warren's population to grow and change without the PCs' direct contribution. This is also a useful move for connecting one chapter to the next. It changes life in the warren and can help set the stage for the coming chapter.

RETIRE

When you give up the ghost or the spotlight, hold 1 and describe how your rabbit retires from play, then make a new rabbit. The hold may be spent to give any rabbit an additional Character move.

Retiring a rabbit means allowing their story to come to an end. This is a normal part of a rabbit's life in *The Warren*—embrace it. This could mean letting them die or it could mean having them take on a more static role in the fiction. Whatever you choose, this is your chance to write your character's fate into the warren's history and leave your mark on the rabbits that survive you.

The retiring rabbit's player retains the hold—they may opt to spend it immediately to aid another PC, spend it to introduce their new rabbit with an additional Character move, or save it for a rainy day.

ADVANCEMENT

During play, each PC may take one additional Character move each chapter as they learn, grow, or change. The move cannot be one already claimed by another character.

When you claim this move, mark it on your rabbit playbook. If you haven't claimed it by the end of the chapter, do it at that time.

I know that you are bigger than I am and can run faster, but I am here to learn what you know, and I will press you with all the means in my power until you tell me.

Richard Adams, Tales from Watership Down

Panicking

Panicking can ruin the best-laid plans and seal the fate of an individual rabbit or even that of a whole warren. When you panic, you're in a bad spot.

When a PC reaches their maximum Panic—usually as a result of a few failed Resist Panic moves—they temporarily lose control and the GM gets to decide which of the rabbit's instincts takes hold: Fight, Flight, or Fright.

▦ FIGHT

You flail wildly, kicking and biting any nearby—or—You see red and attack regardless of consequence.

▦ FLIGHT

You run blindly until you are alone—or—You flee into unconsciousness.

▦ FRIGHT

You freeze, unable to move or even cry out—or—You scream uncontrollably.

A rabbit that succumbs to panic is a rabbit at its most vulnerable. Without help, they are at everyone's mercy and no one needs roll to act against them—the GM will simply narrate the outcomes of any actions taken by PCs or NPCs. A panicked rabbit that is neither injured nor threatened will eventually regain their wits all on their own but not until the situation changes and the GM gives the all clear.

The Help/Hinder move can be useful for restoring a panicked rabbit's senses. When another rabbit decreases a panicked rabbit's Panic score, they immediately come to their senses and their player regains control. Of course, a malicious rabbit might also use Help/Hinder to increase another rabbit's Panic score, thereby causing them to panic!

Fighting

You may notice that, aside from one or two Character moves (such as Tooth and Claw, page 97), there are no moves for directly doing violence—this is an intentional omission! Only a few rabbits will be big, mean, or experienced enough for violence to be a go-to option. Most rabbits will have to be clever to survive and get their way.

Does this mean you can't do violence? No, but it does mean that you have to say what your rabbit does and that the GM gets to decide what happens. A clever rabbit will do all they can to make sure that the situation they create points toward their victory.

Here are some guidelines for resolving potentially violent situations:

If two or more PCs are fighting, this most likely triggers the Compete move (page 37).

If an NPC is attacking the PC, it's a GM move (see page 56). This will probably start with a soft move followed by asking what the PC does next.

If the PC wants to fight an NPC, the GM should ask them how do they do it. Do they have a relevant move that is triggered? If not, it's up to the GM to decide the outcome.

Has the PC set up a favorable situation or is this pure folly? Let them just do the violence or treat it as a golden opportunity to make a hard move, respectively.

As the GM, keep an eye out for other moves that may be used to resolve the situation. Is the PC starting the fight with threats? Consider using Speak Plainly and determine the outcome from there. Maybe you say, "Hindpaw is no runt, you can drive him off if you can keep your nerve up—roll to Resist Panic" or "You get in a good nip but Hindpaw lunges forward, pinning your ear to the ground—are you going to Struggle free?"

Whatever methods you use, keep in mind that looking for a fight is always going to be dicey.

Scars

Any rabbit of sufficient age bears the physical and psychological scars of a lifetime of hardship and predation. Player characters accumulate scars when a move calls for them to gain a scar or when physical or mental trauma follows from the fiction. Non-player characters may be injured or even slain when a player's move calls for it or when the fiction dictates they should die.

When a PC gains a scar, they must pick one Basic or Character move (but not a Special move) that they may no longer make, based on the nature of the wound. They should cross the lost move off of their rabbit playbook and describe how the injury relates to the lost move.

Moves that are crossed off are no longer available to that character. If a Character move is crossed off in this manner, it is immediately available for other rabbits to take as their advance for the session. No rabbit may reclaim a move during the same chapter in which they lost that move.

Whenever a lost move would normally be triggered, the GM will treat it as though they rolled a 6- and make a GM move as a result. Importantly, triggering a lost move doesn't mean that the PC's action fails but it does mean that the situation will become more dire. Players should be on the lookout for situations where lost moves would otherwise be triggered and accept the consequences of a 6- or choose a different course of action.

With the dog getting closer and closer, Barley would dearly like to run but he's in no shape to do so since I crossed off the Bolt move. Instead, Barley is going to press himself low to the ground behind the jalopy's rear tire and hope the dog doesn't notice him—that's a Sneak move, right?

Gaining a scar need not be the end of a rabbit. Losing a move or three in this manner can make for a fun creative constraint and playing to past traumas can make for excellent fiction. However, a PC's scars will begin to slow them down—when a PC has three or more scars, consider retiring the rabbit.

Retirement

Someday when I get older and slower, my own
life cycle will end. I may become the prey of the
owl or the fox. Those foolish crows will laugh
over my bones. They won't have the last laugh,
though, because one of my descendants will
look up into the trees and chuckle when they see
those hilarious birds.

Amy Griffin Ouchley, Swamper:
Letters from a Louisiana Swamp Rabbit

In a one-shot game, retiring a rabbit can make for high drama and become the pivotal moment of the game. In a multi-chapter game, character turnover makes for good games by telling more of the warren's stories. Retiring your rabbit also means that your Character moves go back into the pool for others to choose. Sometimes players will want to have a dramatic death scene or take a fated action to ensure that their death counts for something. A rabbit's death needn't be described in detail—maybe they lead a predator off into the tall grass, never to be heard from again.

▦ RETIRE

When you give up the ghost or the spotlight, hold 1 and describe how your rabbit retires from play, then make a new rabbit. The hold may be spent to give any rabbit an additional Character move.

Player characters can also be retired when their player opts to let them adopt a more static role in the fiction. They become another member of the warren. While retired rabbits are no longer under the control of a player, they will always be a rabbit of note within the warren because of their relationships and past deeds.

Once a PC is retired, the GM is free to use them as an NPC and any Character moves they possessed are immediately available for other rabbits take when they advance. The player is also free to create a new PC to play—preferably a rabbit that already has ties to the existing fiction. Perhaps they will play a young rabbit just coming of age, an adult rabbit that has not yet played a role in the fiction, or perhaps a rabbit from another warren already established in the fiction.

Running the Game

*Ideas are like rabbits. You get a couple
and learn how to handle them,
and pretty soon you have a dozen.*

John Steinbeck

Being the Game Master

When you run a game of *The Warren*, it is your job as GM to help
shape the fiction. Whether you are GMing a single session, a whole
series of sessions, or are just taking your turn to act as GM, the
following section is addressed to the GM and explains the tools
and procedures you need to fill in the world around the other
players' characters.

You do that by creating threats, predators, and NPCs and playing
them according to your principles and agendas. You will also shape
the fiction by setting the tone, describing locations and situations,
making GM moves that players must react to, and by helping to
interpret the outcomes of characters' actions.

Agendas

GMs in *The Warren* have three distinct agendas during play. These agendas are your ultimate goals; you aren't here to do anything else.

Always:

- Portray a naturalistic world.
- Ensure the characters live in exciting times.
- Play to find out.

Portray a Naturalistic World

The Warren is not a game of pulp adventure or a fairy tale. As a GM it is your job to describe all that surrounds the PCs. In doing so, you should show them the world, holistically and unflinchingly, as it is. That means that every character is dynamic and fallible and every choice has real-world consequences. The world around them is beautiful and terrible and often indifferent.

Ensure the Characters Live in Exciting Times

Regardless of when or where the warren in your game is located, rabbits will always be on the bottom of the food chain. A rabbit's world is filled with uncertainty and danger. It is a world of low places to hide and exposed areas to brave. As a GM, it is your job to portray an ever-changing world filled with threats from without and within the warren.

Play to Find Out

Embrace the world's uncertainty and play to find out what will become of the warren. You should never try to plan out the course of events or guess at what the PCs will do. As a GM, it is your job to discover the fiction along with your players.

Principles

In addition to the three agendas, GMs in *The Warren* also have a set of principles which guide them as they uphold their side of the conversation. If agendas are *what* you should be doing, then principles are *how* you should be doing it.

- Address yourself to the characters, not the players.
- Create interesting situations, not plots.
- Build a bigger world through play.
- Ask questions, build on the answers.
- Make your move but never speak its name.
- Make the world seem real using all senses.
- Look at your non-player animals and ideas through crosshairs.
- Name every animal.
- Be a fan of the characters.
- Think off-screen, too.
- Tell players what humans do but interpret their actions for the rabbits.

Address Yourself to the Characters, Not the Players

By structuring the conversation as one between you and the characters, you can better keep the focus on the fiction at hand. So, rather than saying, "Jason, what does Clover do?" you would say, "Clover, what do you do?"

So, Barley, are you going to let Pinecone take credit for finding Silver?

Create Interesting Situations, not Plots

It may be tempting to plan a series of events you'd like to play out, a moral you'd like to teach, or a story you'd like to tell—don't. Instead, look for interesting dilemmas, conflicts, and choices to present the PCs so that you can find out what happens. Think of the questions you'd like to see answered in play, but not their answers.

Coriander won't make it back to the warren on her own but you won't reach her litter in the hastily scratched burrow before dawn unless you leave now. What do you do?

Build a Bigger World through Play

Because you aren't planning what should happen in the fiction, you shouldn't be creating all of the details of the setting before you get to the table. It can certainly be helpful to decide some foundational details about the world where your game will take place—just a couple potential locations, NPCs, and situations upon which to anchor further play. Start small! Start with what the rabbits can see from their warren. Then, as you follow the fiction, continue to fill in the setting around the PCs and let their actions and choices dictate how you link and fill in the spaces between the setting elements you've prepared.

Near the warren is a long abandoned mill and, just on the other side of the river, wheat fields stretch all the way to the farmhouse. Aside from the road cutting through it, it's thick forest in every other direction.

Ask Questions, Build on the Answers

You might be apprehensive about starting a game with so little preparation to fall back on—it's okay, you're playing to find out. Fortunately, you're not alone—ask your players when you can't think of something or want to know about something. Questions are a key part of conversation. The most important question is, "What do you do?" You should be asking this all the time. Also, make a habit of turning questions back on players—"What parts of the bridge can you see?" "What have you heard about the rabbits of Montvale Warren?" By sharing some authority over the setting with the players, you will create fiction that they care about.

What tracks have you seen the last couple times you've come to the river?

Make your Move but Never Speak its Name

Each GM move (see the next section) is an archetypal way of advancing the fiction. These moves are a structure, which rely on you to add your own fictional details before implementing them in the fiction. So, rather than saying, "I separate them," you would say, "The dog dashes between you and pauses, unsure which of you to pursue." Each of the GM moves provides you with an appropriate way of complicating the PCs' lives and goading a response from them.

The corn snake pauses at the mouth of the warren, looking in. Fennel, you can see it looking at you but Lily is stuck outside.

Make the World Seem Real Using all Senses

Rabbits are exquisitely sensory creatures; they must be to survive. Make sure to insert details involving all of a rabbit's senses into the fiction. Say what is seen, smelled, tasted. Say what is heard, felt, and intuited. Show the world from the rabbit's perspective—close to or under the ground, surrounded by signs of potential danger.

Sniffing around the brush, you know it's a rabbit but not one you've ever encountered before.

Look at Your Non-Player Characters and Ideas through Crosshairs

As a GM, you have broad powers to introduce elements into the fiction. These elements are in no way privileged—be ready to let them go. Your contributions exist to interact with, build upon, and be destroyed. For rabbits, nothing is safe or stable for long. Don't worry; you'll have plenty more opportunities to contribute elements you find interesting.

Captain Thorn's eyes go wide as he realizes that you've left him no escape from the backyard, the barks no longer muffled by the closed patio door.

Name Every Character

It is important to remember that all animals, including humans, are people. As such, they have their own names, agendas, proclivities, and dispositions. Naming them also gives the character an anchor in the fiction and players' memories so that characters can be reincorporated later. Unused names from the rabbit playbook can be used to name rabbit NPCs. For other animals, look to their anatomy, sounds, habitats, and cultures for names.

Nice to meet you, I'm Saltgrass. Name's Thistle. They call me Squeak. Just Sandy's fine.

Be a Fan of the Characters

In *The Warren*, the PCs are the main characters and much of the fiction will be experienced from their perspective. As a GM, it isn't your job to ensure they succeed, try to best them, or get them to act in any particular way. Sit back and experience the fiction with them as you would with the main character of your favorite TV show or novel—grin when they overcome a challenge and grimace when harm befalls them, watch them change and grow, and enjoy their interesting lives. Look for chances to let them shine and use their unique moves.

My heart goes out to you but you were there, Long Ears said you weren't welcome here anymore. Best get a move on before Slobber figures out you doubled back.

Look, that rabbit's got a vicious streak a mile wide! It's a killer!

Tim the Enchanter, Monty Python and the Holy Grail

Think Off-screen, Too

Not everything in the fiction happens where the PCs can experience it right away. During play, think about other things that are going on in the setting. When you make a GM, threat, or predator move that happens somewhere else, consider what effect it might have on the PCs' current location or situation or how its effects might first make themselves known to the PCs. Look for ways to foreshadow the unrevealed change in the fiction.

You see a flash almost immediately followed by thunder, and in the light you finally see the path through the tall, dry grass leading back to the warren.

Tell Players What Humans Do but Interpret Their Actions for the Rabbits

Human behavior and technology may forever be a mystery to animals—that doesn't mean it has to be confusing for players. When you describe the actions a human is taking, for example driving away in a car, tell the players what is happening so that they can imagine it for themselves. However, remember that you should also be addressing the PC, who is a rabbit. Describe the human's actions the way an animal might experience them or use the colloquialisms you've already established in play.

Farmer McGrath fires up the old tractor but what you hear is the awakening of the thunderous monster whose return your mother foretold.

GM Moves

As discussed earlier (page 24), GM moves are a set of tools that the GM can use to push the fiction along or get it going in a new direction. GM moves are typically made when a character rolls a 6-, when players ignore an imminent threat, or when the players look to you to say what happens next.

- Reveal an impending threat.
- Separate them.
- Pin them down.
- Put someone in a spot.
- Introduce a predator.
- Add to their Panic.
- Scar them.
- Announce off-screen badness.
- Give them a difficult decision to make.
- Give an opportunity, consequence, or both.
- Turn their move back on them.
- Use a threat or predator move.

Soft and Hard Moves

Each of these GM moves can be played either "soft" or "hard." Soft moves introduce a threat or complication—something that the PCs can respond to, overcome, or avoid. Soft moves escalate a current situation or foreshadow future hardship but do not impose irrevocable consequences.

Hard moves, on the other hand, introduce the hardship or consequence itself—something that the PCs have to respond to, suffer, or lose.

In general, you'll want to start with soft moves and escalate toward hard moves when PCs ignore an imminent danger or when their moves result in further 6- die rolls.

⊞ REVEAL AN IMPENDING THREAT

It hasn't affected them yet but it will if they don't do something to change the situation. This is probably the move that you will use the most.

As the rain pounds the earth outside, the water in the burrow begins to rise.

⊞ SEPARATE THEM

Whether in a maze of tunnels or out in a pasture, it's easy to get separated during a crisis. Sometimes it will be a predator forcing them apart but it could just as easily be a social system coming between them. When a rabbit is cut off from the help of other rabbits, this is one way to put them on the spot but also a chance to put them in the spotlight. Splitting the rabbits into different groupings can also spotlight relationships.

As Holly is led off down the run, Eyetooth's enforcers step in to block the entrance to the burrow. What do you do?

⊞ PIN THEM DOWN

Sometimes there's just nowhere to run. Whether they're holed up in a burrow or lying motionless beneath a bush, this is a good way to put the action on hold. It can provide a chance for rabbits to talk or it can put things on pause while you find out what another rabbit is doing.

Mrs. Farmer comes around the shed with her gun; if you move she'll have Sumac in her sights for sure—Ivy, what are you doing?

⊞ PUT SOMEONE IN A SPOT

Putting them in a spot means endangering them or something they care about in a way that demands immediate action. Whether it's running, fighting, speaking up, or struggling to get free, what they do right now will stick.

"Oh?…and I suppose you're volunteering," Ember says, as all eyes turn to look at you.

⊞ INTRODUCE A PREDATOR

No matter where rabbits are, predators abound. No matter what rabbits are doing, predators mean trouble.

Suddenly, stoats.

⊞ ADD TO THEIR PANIC

Even the bravest and steadiest rabbits can succumb to panic. When rabbits do something that exposes them to danger or stress, tell them to Resist Panic. When things don't go the way the PCs planned, say how and either tell them to Resist Panic or outright increase their Panic, depending on whether you're making this as a soft or hard move.

Panic plays an important role in Birthing a Litter. An unusually low roll or unusually high Panic score when Birthing a Litter often results in both a small litter and the GM getting to make a move. When this happens, feel free to use your move to mix and match fictional consequences with increases in Panic to the doe or any others that are present.

This litter is going to take longer than you thought. You're doing your best to help the doe but the strain is wearing on you—you should roll to Resist Panic.

⊞ SCAR THEM

There is danger all around and sometimes rabbits get hurt. Choose a looming threat that has been established in the fiction and tell them what it does to scar them (see Scars, page 45).

There's a loud bang and something hits you in the flank, flipping you over. You feel a searing pain and the smell of blood is all around you—take a scar.

⊞ ANNOUNCE OFF-SCREEN BADNESS

Not all threats are clear or immediate. A clue or rumor, a sign or scent may not seem like much now but can foreshadow events that will be revealed later.

The wind shifts and for a moment you smell smoke but then it is gone. What do you do?

⊞ GIVE THEM A DIFFICULT DECISION TO MAKE

Three is a dangerous number. Involve an NPC to drive conflict between two PCs. Pit two NPCs or threats against one another and make the PCs choose which to address. Allow two threats to coincide and let them decide which to confront.

"If we are going to thrive as a warren, Ragweed and her followers must go. Are you with us or with them?"

⊞ GIVE AN OPPORTUNITY, CONSEQUENCE, OR BOTH

It pays to be direct. Tell them the consequences for an action and ask if they are willing to accept them. Give them an opportunity but tell them what it will cost them. Sometimes, just give them an opportunity and figure out the ramifications later.

You can rescue Old One Ear but it means going out into the open where you're totally exposed—you'll have to resist panicking.

⊞ TURN THEIR MOVE BACK ON THEM

Give them exactly what they wanted but not the way they wanted it. Maybe they are betrayed, maybe there is a hidden cost, maybe what they wanted just isn't all it was cracked up to be.

You run harder than you ever have before and you do reach the hole in the fence but, turning back, you see Copper far behind and the dog is closing fast.

⊞ USE A THREAT OR PREDATOR MOVE

Both threats and predators include appropriate moves that the GM may use when the PCs interact with them. Sometimes these will be specific instances of GM moves but other times they are simply things that occur in the fiction.

Barley can't make it in time and the hawk swoops down and snatches her, digging its claws deep into her haunches.

Threats, Predators, and NPCs

Threats, predators, and NPCs are named elements of your setting that will be focal points in the fiction. They are generally created outside of play, in preparation for a session. If you are using one of the existing World playsets (see page 79) these elements will already be included for you.

Threats

In *The Warren*, a threat represents an important or dynamic aspect of your fiction's setting. Your game might have a Threat of Harvest, Threat of Haystack Warren, Threat of Cottontail's Ascendancy, or any other aspect of your fiction that is moving in an important direction.

For the GM, threats act as touchstones, organizing the fiction around important details and helping to prepare moves that reincorporate and maintain the existing themes.

The Threat of Highway

Intent: To divide the land

- Men arrive to survey the land
- Machines ravage the pasture
- Trucks leave piles of dirt and gravel
- Four lanes threaten any who cross

Predators

Within their ecosystem, rabbits are prey to every predator bigger than they are and some that aren't. Young rabbits are particularly vulnerable. Predators are a constant threat to rabbits caught in the open but some may even threaten the warren itself.

Occasionally, a particularly large or mean rabbit might even be considered a predator. Humans can, at times, be predators (see page 98).

Poison, disease, snares, and other environmental hazards are just as much of a danger to rabbits as any animal. These types of dangers should be written up and played the same as predators in your prep.

SAX, the Fox

Trait: Curious

Voice: Charming, Upper-class

- Disappear and reappear elsewhere, seemingly at random
- Bite and hold, playfully considering what to do
- Follow at a distance, biding his time
- Entice them and make any number of assurances
- Hold a grudge, for now, forever

NPCs

There are other characters in the game besides the players' characters and the predators who hunt them. These non-player characters (NPCs) include other rabbits in the warren as well as nearby animals who have their own personalities, problems, and agendas.

NPCs are written exactly like predators, with a name, personality traits, voices, and moves.

NETTLE, Hedgehog

Trait: Sneaky

Voice: High and Sniffly

- Roll into a spiney ball
- Call on the extended family
- Give dogs pause, the second time
- Hibernate in winter

Making Threats

When you make a threat, write it out on a note card. threats have three main parts: a name, an intent, and moves.

Name

Start by giving the threat a name. It should be relatively straight-forward; for example, The threat of Kudzu or The threat of Spring. Write it in big letters so it's one of the first things you see when you look down.

Intent

Next, write down the threat's intent. A threat's intent describes the end toward which the threat is moving. A threat's intent doesn't have to be a fixed, inevitable end—just the way things will probably go if nothing changes. The Threat of Kudzu might have the intent: To envelop the grove. Threats can also be chained, with one threat leading to the next, e.g. The Threat of Spring might have the intent: To become Summer.

Moves

Lastly, write some moves for the threat. Think of the ways each threat might complicate rabbit's lives. Three to five is a good number. The Threat of Kudzu might have moves like: Leaves blot out the sun, Nest of predators, Dead trees fall, and Humans spray toxic chemicals. The Threat of Spring might have moves like: Thorns grow thick, Cacophony of baby birds, Torrential rains, and Grass grows tall (see more examples on page 87).

Threat moves can be organized to fulfill different types of roles. Some threats, like The Threat of Spring above, will be in play for a whole session and the threat moves will be used as needed. Other threats might have a set of moves that can each be used once.

For example, The Threat of Mystery might have a set of one-time revelations. Give these moves boxes so that you can check them off, in any order, as you use them. Other threats might have moves that are meant to be made in order. For example, The Threat of Thistle's

Peril might have a set of worsening circumstances that result in his demise. Give these moves numbers so that you can cross them off as you narrate them in the fiction.

Using Threats in Play

Before your first chapter, think about three or four threats that might be interesting to put in the game. Then, as you ask questions at the table and begin developing the setting, incorporate threats that fit the unfolding story. They don't need to be fully fleshed out— you can fill in the intent and moves as you think of them.

Some good threats to make during creation of a rabbit warren include: a threat for whoever is unhappy with the way things are in the warren, a threat for the greatest danger to the warren, or a threat for a notable location near the warren. Exchange one or two of the threats you had on hand for ones that relate to the way the players answer the first chapter questions.

During play, feel free to modify threats as you go. If you think up a useful move for a threat, add it to the existing ones. If one of the threat's moves no longer gels with the fiction, remove it.

threats are dynamic and will not last forever. Sometimes you will mark off all of the threat's moves or the players can't or won't do anything to change the course of events. At this point, the threat's intent has come to fruition and should be considered part of the fiction. You may still find an opportunity to use its moves, for example The Threat of Kudzu will still be as deep and dark as ever, but the kudzu will have fully enveloped the grove and will become a static element in the fiction.

Sometimes threats will become less relevant. Maybe you just want to jump ahead in the fiction without discovering whether the threat achieves its intent. When this happens, you should retire the threat. Set it aside and let its presence in the fiction fade into the background. However, don't discard the threat card—it may become relevant again or you may want to reintroduce it later.

Making Predators

Predators in *The Warren* are made up of three components: a name, personality traits, a voice, and predator moves.

Name

When you make a predator, name it. For some animals, simply list the animal's species. However, for predators that have a larger place in the fiction, you can also list the animal's name.

Personality Traits

Remember, all animals in *The Warren*, even predators, are intelligent and possess their own personality. Even if they have no interest in conversing with rabbits, this trait is what makes them more than a nameless, faceless monster (even if that's how they usually behave). If you haven't introduced the predator into the fiction yet, consider listing two or three traits so that you can pick whichever one seems most appropriate in the moment.

Voice

The best way to express the predator's personality is through its voice. Does it speak slowly or quickly? Is it high or low? When in doubt, think of celebrities or people you know to quickly give the predator more character. In the example to the right, the hound dog Buddy has a deep voice and a slow-witted demeanor.

Moves

Next, give it predator moves appropriate to its species and nature. Think about the physical characteristics and behaviors that the predator has evolved and how they might be used to harm, harry, or horrify a rabbit. Three to five moves should do.

Using Predators in Play

Predators will usually enter into the fiction in one of two ways. The first is that you will introduce a predator as one of your GM moves. The players will roll a 6-, ignore an obvious threat, or simply give you the "Well, what now?" look and there it will be—a hawk's shadow, the hum of a motor, the scent of a fox, or the spray of dirt from a bullet that landed altogether too close for comfort.

The second, considerably less likely way is that players will either introduce them into the fiction themselves or, even more foolhardy, their PCs will actually seek out a predator. Perhaps they seek to make an offering, a bribe, or show of force. Perhaps they think to lay a trap, lure them into harm's way, or lead them into an enemy warren. No matter, introducing the predator will follow from the fiction and you should keep an eye out for opportunities to make a soft or hard move and add a predator to their situation.

Predators and Harm

Occasionally, predators themselves will come to harm. Sometimes it will come directly from the PCs, for example if one of them has the Tooth and Claw Character move. Other times, PCs may be able to indirectly harm a predator through careful fictional positioning, for example luring it into a trap or leading it to an even nastier predator. Sometimes, it will simply follow from the fiction. If a predator is wounded, mark off one or more moves. If a predator has no moves left or if the fiction demands it, then the predator may die or find itself helpless, at the mercy of all.

BUDDY, Hound Dog

Trait: Lazy

Voice: Deep and slow-witted

- Bark and bark and bark
- Give chase
- Bite and shake
- Sniff out a trail
- Widen an existing hole

Establishing the Tone

One of the GM's jobs is to help the group establish the tone of the game. As explained earlier (page 17), you should have a discussion about setting, theme, and tone before the game begins. Will your story be heroic or tragic? Will it focus on grim realism or will it be more fanciful?

By default *The Warren* is a lyrical and surprisingly gentle game, genuinely suitable for all ages. There will be danger and hardship, but to a very large degree the fate of your dear rabbit is in your hands. Death is omnipresent but unlikely to befall you unless you decide it is time.

This is a wonderful mode of play, but it is possible to approach it with a harder edge, where the notion of winning by outbreeding your enemies takes center stage and life is all too short. With a table full of adults committed to the idea of a darker tone, it can be intense and very, very fun.

Playing with Dark Mode

Are you ready for Dark Mode? Some advice before taking the leap:

Players, don't get too attached to your characters, because the game isn't about them—the game is about the warren. Individual rabbits are cheap and the continuity of the warren is everything. Death is explicitly on the table and will occur as the fiction demands, so breed early and often. Your kits are your legacy (and the pool from which you will probably draw your next character).

Think of the game as a generational saga rather than an heroic narrative. Although your characters may well be leaders, poets, and scofflaws, they are still at the bottom of the food chain in a world determined to kill them. Perhaps their children can finish what you so bravely started. Generational play is great fun, and having a strong connection to the warren as a living community pays great dividends over time. You'll start to care about its health and goals, and build a mythology around the exploits of previous generations. And, despite all these lofty assurances, in the end making up a new rabbit takes only minutes.

GMs, all the agenda and principle items still apply. There are two principles that you really need to pay attention to in Dark Mode. "Look at your non-player animals and ideas through crosshairs" should always be on your mind, and you should be ruthless. Have scouting parties not return. Have rabbits die in childbirth, or from disease. "Be a fan of the characters," perhaps ironically, becomes even more important in a Dark Mode game. Even though life is cheap and death may come early, even if a player's investment doesn't rise above erasing one name and writing in another, never forget that you are at the table to make each other awesome. The PCs are heroes, so make sure their kits have stories to tell, even if those stories end with them sacrificing their lives for the warren.

Like your agenda and principles, all the GM moves apply as usual in Dark Mode, but what constitutes soft and hard can be modified a little. "Add to their Panic" barely qualifies as a GM move in Dark Mode—you should keep them scared, and adding Panic is the softest move you can make. Hand it out like rabbit chow in a meat hutch. "Reveal an impending threat" and "announce off-screen badness" can both directly result in dead NPCs. "Scar them" is axiomatic in Dark Mode. Have less mercy and think bigger picture in general. Of course these are just suggestions that you'll naturally adjust to taste.

If you think this sounds fun, make sure your entire group is on board with a game that will skew pretty bleak, with all animals—no matter how innocent—being regularly imperiled, injured, and killed. If the entire group isn't unified in its enthusiasm, just play the regular game. Even if they are excited about a darker tone, keep the X-Card (see page 109) handy and be prepared to dial the intensity back, which you can do easily if necessary.

Telling the Story

*A **man who chases two rabbits catches none.***

Proverb

The First Chapter

Gameplay in *The Warren* is broken up into a series of chapters. The first chapter is especially important because it is when the players and the GM will describe the World around their warren and breathe life into the rabbits within it.

Before you begin play, your group should decide whether you'll be using one of the established World playsets (see page 79) or creating your own setting by answering the default setting questions on the next page.

Either way, you'll ask and answer questions about your warren, your relationships, and the situation in the first chapter of your story.

Subsequent chapters will build on the first, generally following the same structure—increasingly specific questions that establish an interesting situation, following the PCs' actions and their consequences to find out what happens, and identifying a point in the conversation to let things settle so that the next chapter takes the warren's story in a new direction.

Default Setting Questions

Once the players have created their PCs, keep the conversation going by finding out about the setting and the initial situation as the chapter begins. You do this by asking the players a series of questions. The questions range from very broad contextual questions to very specific situational questions. You needn't ask all the questions but pick a couple from each category. Prompt them for additional details until you are satisfied with the answer to each question and can picture it vividly in your mind.

If you are using an established World playset, use those questions instead.

Warren Questions

Warren questions help to establish the specifics of the warren that will be the focus of the game. These questions set up general situations and help everyone share in imagining the warren, its inhabitants, and its surroundings. Pose these questions to the players as a whole or to individual PCs. Consider asking the same question to more than one PC if you think there might be more than one correct answer.

- What directions and landmarks would a rabbit give to locate the warren?
- What can you see as you look out from the warren?
- Is the warren large, small, or somewhere in between?
- How was the warren founded?
- Who are its revered personages, living or dead?
- What do your senses tell you about the warren?
- How are decisions made in the warren?
- Who's unhappy about the way things are in the warren?
- What is your place in the warren?
- What threat will destroy the warren if left unchecked?
- What is the hardest thing for rabbits in the warren to obtain?
- What might others covet about the warren?
- What would make the warren a better place?
- What _____?

Relationship Questions

Loner or leader, mother or newcomer, no matter what a rabbit's standing in the warren is, they know at least one other rabbit. Pose relationship questions to individual rabbits and their answers can specify other PCs or NPCs. Take note of any new NPCs the players mention.

- Who do you trust most of all?
- Who makes your life miserable?
- Who do you wish was your mate?
- Who have you let sleep in your burrow?
- Who's the oldest rabbit you know?
- Who has turned out to be your rival?
- Who would you like to see in charge?
- Whose shadow have you been living in?
- Who knows your secret?
- Who _____?

Situational Questions

Each chapter of *The Warren* starts out in the middle of the action rather than during life as usual. Pose situational questions to individual PCs.

- Is it day or night or somewhere between?
- Why are you all away from the warren?
- When did you realize you were lost?
- Who is hurt or trapped?
- What animal just approached you?
- What predator has just revealed itself?
- What _____?

Always Ask

- What do you do?

Stakes Questions

Stakes questions are questions that the GM asks themself and hopes to answer during a chapter. You don't need to choose stakes questions before the session begins; instead, settle on one or two after play has begun and let them guide the direction of the fiction.

- What happens when rabbits are born?
- What happens when rabbits die?
- What things do they prize in the warren?
- What happens when a new rabbit arrives?
- What relationship will the warren have with other warrens?
- What predators terrorize the warren?
- What other animals live nearby?
- What problems do humans cause?
- What will happen if the rabbits are driven from the warren?
- What happens when a rabbit's station in the warren changes?
- What _____?

The rabbit has a charming face:
Its private life is a disgrace.
I really dare not name to you
The awful things that rabbits do.

Anonymous

Ending a Chapter

All chapters come to an end. You'll know it's a good time to end a chapter when you can finish the following phrase:

...and that's how _____.

Good times to consider completing this phrase and ending the chapter are when:

- A threat resolves.
- A stakes question is answered.
- An important character dies.
- An important character births a litter.
- PCs triumph over a predator.
- PCs achieve an important goal.
- You run out of time to play.

It's usually better to end a chapter a little early than to let it drag on a little too long. Be sure to remind characters who have not taken a new Character move as advancement to do so at the end of the chapter.

Remember, chapters need not conform to sessions. You can always end a chapter and begin a new one after a quick break or continue a chapter next session.

If you plan to play another chapter, take a moment to note any unanswered questions that remain and add some new questions about the fiction in preparation for the next chapter.

Subsequent Chapters

Each chapter is a piece of the warren's history. Many games will last only one chapter but you may want to continue the warren's story though a series of chapters.

Because the fiction will always take place during interesting times for the warren, weeks or months may separate chapters. If time has passed since the last chapter, make the Special move Time Goes By (see page 41).

A warren's population is always in flux. Each new chapter is a chance to add new players or characters. If any rabbits birthed a litter in the last chapter, their kits may now be out on their own as well, possibly as new PCs.

If any players retired their rabbits in the previous chapter, they may be holding an option to give someone a new Character move.

For the remaining PCs, have them reset their Panic score to zero at the start of play.

When a new chapter picks up you should again use questions to get the fiction rolling again.

At the table:

- Ask any questions you have prepared.
- Ask about the PCs and the animals they love and scorn.
- Ask about any threats from the last chapter and move at least one of them closer to its intent (see Threats on page 60).
- Ask situational questions to start characters in the thick of it.
- Ask "What do you do?"

Some Facts About Rabbits

- Rabbits are not hares but jackrabbits are.

- Rabbits mark territory with droppings, spray, and scent glands on their chins.

- Young rabbits are submissive and docile.

- Adults form competitive hierarchies among rabbits of their own gender.

- Rabbits groom warren members and thump the ground with their hind legs to warn of danger.

- Rabbits are thought to have evolved from the alilepus, a giant rabbit-like creature.

- Swamp rabbits are excellent swimmers and the only species wherein males are larger than females.

- Three species of rabbit can climb trees.

- Young rabbits are called "kits" or "kitlings" and can last only two days without milk until weaned.

- European rabbits produce about 360 "pellets" per day.

- Rabbits can transmit the plague, tularemia, and Rocky Mountain spotted fever.

- Humans have carried rabbits' feet for luck for 1,500 years.

- Rabbits have five forepaw toes and four hindpaw toes.

- Female rabbits have two uteri.

Worlds

The rabbit has an evil mind,
Although he looks so good and kind,
His life is a complete disgrace,
Although he has so soft a face.
I hardly like to let you know
How far his wickedness will go.

Anonymous, *Canine Capers*

World Playsets

Worlds are established collections of ideas, questions, threats, predators, NPCs, and custom moves related to a specific setting that you bring to the table—a crib sheet to help you anchor gameplay to the setting and themes you hope to focus on.

If you're looking for a quick and easy setting for your game, maybe one you can just pull out of your bag and get started with right away, then consider using one of the premade Worlds on the following pages or one of the many World playsets available for *The Warren* at the Bully Pulpit Games website.

You can also use these as examples and create your own Worlds based on the times and places you'd like to explore or the settings close to your heart that you'd like to share. If you do, let us know, we'd love to see them!

World of Abingdon Meadow

Written by Marshall Miller

The fallow meadow lies nearby the town of Abingdon, a short ways down a narrow county road. Stories tell of a time when the meadow was planted with barley but the overgrown meadow has long since gone to seed. Humans still come to hunt for rabbits caught out in the open but at least they've let the warren be. Very little has happened in the warren since the time of barley. The hedgerows are as they ever were and the same predators worry the warren that did a generation ago.

Names

Hedgerow Foliage:

Hawthorn, Blackthorn, Holly, Ivy, Hazel, Dogwood, Dead Wood, Honeysuckle, Blackberry, Field Maple

Warren Rabbits:

Rosemary, Aster, Thistle, Sedge, Cress, Boxwood, Heath, Snowflake, Foxglove, Primrose

Other Rabbits:

Buttercup, Knotgrass, Sorrel, Bracken, Dorset, Poppy, Sundew, Birch, Adler, Bounder

Birds:

Tawny Owl, Woodpecker, Rook, Jackdaw, Warbler, Wren, Starling, Thrush, Honey Buzzard, Sparrowhawk, Eddy, Balmy, Aurora, Cirrus, Pileus, Parhelion, Nimbus, Muggy, Isobar, Squall

Other Creatures:

Stoat, Badger, Weasel, Roe Deer, Pine Martin, Brown Rat, Feral Cat, Red Squirrel, Mountain Hare, The Hungry Tunnel

Questions: The Warren

- What part of the meadow marks the warren's location?
- How much of the vast warren goes unused and uninhabited?
- What do your senses tell you about the warren?
- What is the one story everyone in the warren knows and who tells it best?
- Why aren't you in charge of the warren?
- What might others covet about the warren?
- Before Cottontail, how many winters had it been since the warren last saw a newcomer?

Questions: Relationship

- Who makes your life miserable?
- Who do you wish was your mate?
- Who have you let sleep in your burrow?
- Who's the oldest rabbit you know?
- Who has turned out to be your rival?
- Who would you like to see in charge?

Questions: Situation

- Is it day or night or somewhere between?
- Why are you all so far away from the warren?
- How did the hunters get between you and the warren?
- What other animal shares your hiding spot?

Questions: Stakes

- What do they do when rabbits die?
- What will happen when, by chance, a tunnel connects with another warren?
- What will happen if the rabbits are driven from the warren?

...What do you do?

Custom Moves

⊞ NOSE AROUND

When you start asking questions, roll+Shrewd. On a 10+, choose two. On a 7-9, choose one:

- You get answers to your questions.
- You're sure no one witnessed your inquiries.
- You don't answer any of their questions.

⊞ LOST

When you try to find your way in a strange warren, roll+Shrewd. On a 10+, you make your way to your intended destination. On a 7-9, you find your way to the surface but you'll have to find another way down if you hope to find your destination.

Some Facts About Rabbits

- Rabbits have variously been observed to form monogamous bonds, mate opportunistically, and engage in serial monogamy.

- A seasoned warren in Australia was found to contain 500 meters of tunnels with over 150 entrances.

- Rabbits fight as fiercely as other animals, biting, scratching, kicking, spraying, leaping and checking—there's usually a home-territory advantage.

- Hunters often set noose snares on rabbit trails, sometimes on a bent branch or sapling, and nets over warren entrances.

- Rabbit Hemorrhagic disease (winter) and myxomatosis (summer) are the two rabbit "plagues." Humans have weaponized both to control rabbit populations.

NPCs

COTTONTAIL, Newcomer Rabbit

Trait: Ambitious

Voice: Trustworthy, Used Car Salesman-like

- Speak up for someone beneath his station
- Idly point out the problems of the warren and its leadership
- Meet with small groups to talk about how things could be
- Stage an increasingly less bloodless coup

WINTERGREEN, Head Rabbit

Trait: Practical

Voice: Calm and Frank Demeanor

- Ask others for their opinion
- Act decisively when her mind is made up
- Delegate, delegate, delegate
- Pause to settle others' disputes

LONGTOOTH, Wintergreen's Father

Trait: Absent

Voice: Cheerful

- Volunteer for whatever the task
- Wait it out till things settle down
- Share a bit of history
- Dress someone down

NETTLE, Hedgehog

Trait: Sneaky

Voice: High and Sniffly

- Roll into a spiny ball
- Call on the extended family
- Give dogs pause, the second time
- Hibernate in winter

Predators

LESLIE AND CADBY, Terriers

Trait: Naive

Voice: Young, Wistful, and British

- Bark and bark and bark
- Give merry chase all around the meadow
- Scruff and shake them with great gaiety
- Sniff out a trail without breaking a constant stream of banter
- Widen an existing hole before crawling right in

SAX, Fox

Trait: Curious

Voice: Unconcerned

- Disappear and reappear somewhere else
- Bite and hold while deciding what to do
- Follow at a distance, biding his time
- Entice them and make assurances

SKREE, Hawk

Trait: Efficient

Voice: Sated

- Swoop from above at blinding speed
- Gouge their flanks with sharp talons
- Tear their ears with a hooked beak
- Snatch them and carry them up and away
- Buffet them with wings

JAKE AND CLYDE, Hunters

Trait: Drunk

Voice: Incomprehensible to Rabbits

- Fire their rifles indiscriminately
- Use spotlights in the dark
- Loose dogs and shout encouragement
- Set clumsy snares

Threats

THE THREAT OF COTTONTAIL'S ASCENDANCY

Intent: To reorder the warren's hierarchy

- Some rabbits are cagey and whisper in groups
- Cottontail's followers barricade tunnels
- Cottontail's followers exile Wintergreen
- Cottontail assigns new social statuses

THE THREAT OF BLAZING SUMMER

Intent: To become Fall

- The day goes on and on and on
- Thick, thick vegetation chokes the low places
- Pastoral views attract humans, their children, and their pets
- Water sources run dry and the earth bakes

THE THREAT OF THE MERGE

Intent: To upset the natural order of things

- Tunnels join, to the digger's surprise
- Guards, scouts, or emissaries are met
- New tunnels are dug and rabbits intermingle
- Popular support swings to new leadership

THE THREAT OF LATE FALL

Intent: To become Winter

- Leaves change color and fall
- Hunters hunt with dogs and lamps
- Surrounding fields lie fallow and empty
- The birds depart leaving only hungry raptors

World of Bayou Dupre

Written by Jason Morningstar

Well, things are tough all over in the bayou, *c'est vrai, c'est vrai 'tit monde.* We all got to stay sharp, because everyone here around wants to eat us. Be alert! *Lâche pas! Lâche pas la patate*, my darlings! Everybody hungry, everybody like a nice piece of rabbit, *c'est vrai.* We got to be smarter than them, and fast, too. We can't swim like the swamp rabbits, but who wants to swim? If we were meant to swim we'd have fins. We can't climb like a squirrel but if we were meant to climb we'd be dumb as rocks like them, *'tit monde!*

Names

Trees:

Willow Oak, Bald Cypress, Water Tupelo, Dwarf Palmetto, Spanish Moss

Big, Lanky Swimming Swamp Rabbits:

Milkweed, Iris, Lineberry, Buttonbrush, Grooveburr, Mulberry, Bittercress, Dewberry, Teaberry, Pansy, Marigold

Egrets, Herons, and Ducks:

Sherwood, Moody, Willis

Rats, Nutria, Squirrels, Muskrats, and Beavers:

Derriel, Bassee, Gosie, Tinch, Dower, Balles, Moxley

Alligators, Rat Snakes, Giant Yellow-bellied Frog-eating Diamondback Water Snakes:

Okhina, Achuffa, Pisa-Tuk, Affetipoa

Questions: The Warren

- What directions would a rabbit give to locate the warren?
- What bayou vista can you see as you look out from the warren?
- Is the warren large, small, or somewhere in between?
- How many generations ago did you cross the Great River?
- Where's the stand of bottomland hardwood, the dry hill of clay, the sleeping bear's den?
- Which rabbit, alive or dead, is revered here?
- What do your senses tell you about the warren?
- How are decisions made in the warren? Who is in charge?
- What is your relationship with the swamp rabbits who were here when your ancestors arrived?

Questions: Relationship

- Who makes your life miserable?
- Who do you wish was your mate?
- Who have you let sleep in your burrow?
- Who's the oldest rabbit you know?
- Who has turned out to be your rival?
- Who's unhappy about the way things are in the warren?

Questions: Situation

- Is it day or night or somewhere between?
- Why are you all away from the warren?
- When did you realize you were lost?
- Who is hurt or trapped?
- Who just approached you—a pelican, an opossum, or a raccoon?
- What predator has just revealed itself? A bobcat? A big snake? Something else?

Questions: Stakes

- What happens when rabbits are born, and when they die?
- What happens when a new rabbit arrives?
- What will happen if the rabbits are driven from the warren?
- What happens when rabbits' status in the warren changes?

...What do you do?

Custom Move

⊞ STARE INTO THE EYES OF THE WHITE KING

When you lock eyes with the White King, roll+Steady. On a 10+, choose 2. On a 7-9, choose 1.

- You can look away
- Your body does what you ask it to
- You don't crave the sweet comfort of the White King's jaws

Some Facts About Rabbits

- Rabbits are obligate coprophages. If you don't know what that means, just forget about it.

- Rabbits have twice as many tastebuds as humans.

- Rabbits' split upper lip helps move foliage into their mouths.

- Rabbits have a nearly 360-degree field of vision.

- Rabbits have 40-50 whiskers.

- A rabbit's home range is 2-10 acres.

- Rabbits do not hibernate.

- Rabbits tolerate dehydration better than camels.

- Rabbits were domesticated 1,000 to 1,500 years ago.

- Rabbits have baby teeth, like we do, but they fall out around the time of birth.

- Rabbits sleep about eight hours each day but sleep is broken into 25 minute naps and they spend about half as much time in REM sleep as humans.

NPCs

DELPHINE, Brown Pelican

Trait: No Nonsense

Voice: Southern Lady

- Beat up a mammal
- Observe from the air
- Scold bad behavior
- Hide something (or someone) in her beak
- Shame cowards and the recalcitrant

BOUPIGNON, Raccoon

Trait: In the Way

Voice: Thick, Cajun

- Eat well
- Act as an intermediary
- Talk in third person
- Tag along, friendly-like
- Share dubious knowledge

THE CAPTAIN, Opossum

Trait: Treacherous

Voice: Tired Abe Vigoda-type

- Smile with needle teeth
- Call in a favor
- Summon his muscle, Monette
- Demand tribute
- Protect his own possum ass

Predators

MONETTE, Bobcat

Trait: Lethal

Voice: Cynical, Nerdish

- Snag in gigantic paws
- Death shake
- Limp from a hunter's wound
- Make a cynical comment
- Back-talk The Captain

AFFETIPOA, "The White King"
Albino Canebrake Rattlesnake

Trait: Enchanting

Voice: Soft-spoken, Bored

His name is Choctaw for "One who enchants and ruins." Five feet long, milky white with bands of gold and red eyes.

- Humor his prey
- Appear out of nowhere
- Sink fangs into warm-blooded flesh and wait
- Sun on a log
- Dazzle with unearthly beauty

HOUSATONIC, Hound Dog

Trait: Stupid

Voice: Idiotic and Shouty

- Bark and bark and bark
- Give chase
- Bite and shake
- Sniff out a trail
- Dig it up and eat it

Threats

THE SWAMP RABBITS

Intent: To drive the warren out of the bayou

- Emissaries arrive with talk of peace
- Soldiers and nutria minions amass across river
- Patrols are ambushed
- The warren is flooded

THE WHITE KING

Intent: To receive tribute and sacrifice

- A messenger arrives with an ultimatum
- The warren is divided
- Enforcers appear
- The White King reigns

THE HUNTER

Intent: To destroy the warren

- The hunter arrives crashing through the swamp
- Housatonic runs free
- A grand council is called, for all are in danger
- The warren is sold out and sacrificed

THE BIG MUDDY

Intent: To drown the world

- The rains come and the ground is wet
- River rises, standing water collects in low places
- Entrances are filled with water as the warren floods
- The world is submerged and everyone is drowned

Appendices

Character Moves

⊞ ACE IN THE HOLE

When you negotiate tight spaces, roll+Shrewd. On a 10+, you lose any pursuers amid the twists and turns. On a 7-9, you gain a significant lead on any pursuers.

⊞ CHARISMATIC

You can always find a rabbit or two that are willing to follow you around and do as you say.

⊞ CIRCLES OF LIFE

The fight for survival makes for some strange bedfellows. When you first use this move, choose another type of animal with which you have history and rapport.

⊞ COCKY

When you boast about your future deeds and your boast proves true, hold 1 (max 3). You can then spend your hold, 1 for 1, to remind yourself and others about your deeds and take -1 Panic.

⊞ COMPOSED

When you Relax, subtract your Steady from your Panic instead of just 1.

⊞ DEAD EYES

You have learned to focus through pain, probably in some terrible warren far away. At any time you can take a scar to return your Panic score to zero.

⊞ DOMINANT

Your influence among members of your warren is based on either fear, lineage, reciprocity, or respect. Choose which one and take +1 forward whenever you Speak Plainly using this influence.

⊞ DULL AND KEEN

One of your senses is dull, but another is almost supernaturally keen to compensate. You can never Pay Attention with the dull one, but treat a 7+ as a 10+ with the keen one.

EMISSARY

You represent another warren and are here as a guest, for now. Answer one question about your home warren from each other player now and hold 3. Holds may be spent, 1 for 1, to reveal further secrets about your home warren or the rabbits that live there.

ENGINEER

When you take time to survey a site, identify a feature of the site and how digging there might turn it to the warren's advantage, take +1 forward when you Dig there.

FERTILE

When you Birth a Litter, choose a number between 2 and 12 instead of rolling.

GILDED CAGE

There are humans that will love and protect you if only you return to live with them. When you take this move, hold 1. When you encounter a human you may spend your hold to say why this human will take you in.

GREYFUR

You are old. When others come to you and seek guidance, give it. They gain +1 forward if they do as you advise.

HUTCHWISE

Raised in a cage or hutch, you are familiar with humans' routines and mysteries. When you Pay Attention to humans, add "Why do humans do that?" to the list of questions you can ask. The GM will tell you a truth and a falsehood—pick whichever is more interesting or useful.

LEADER OF RABBITS

When you take charge and give orders, others take +1 forward when they do as they're told.

MARKED BY THE BLACK RABBIT

When others presume you dead, you're not. Return, injured but alive, at some later time—with an incredible story. Then cross off this move.

⊞ MARKED FOR DEATH

You are ill-fated and everyone knows you won't last long—how will you be remembered? Start with one additional Character move when you make your next rabbit.

⊞ NOT A FIGHTER

When you mate with a rabbit, you retain your +1 to Help/Hinder them forever.

⊞ NOT SCARED OF YOU

When you take this move, hold 1. When you encounter a predator you may spend your hold to say how you've bested this type of predator before. You no longer have to Resist Panic when you deal with this type of predator.

⊞ NURTURER

When you give another rabbit your undivided attention, you can reduce their Panic score by 2 when you Help them.

⊞ QUITE THE PAIR

You may play an additional rabbit but only one of the two may advance each chapter.

⊞ SEER

When you have a vision of things to come, ask everyone at the table to contribute a single word about your vision. Describe your vision, taking care to include those words. The GM may ask you additional questions about it and then they will incorporate your vision into the fiction.

⊞ SENSE OF SPACE

You've ranged near and far and if anyone knows the lay of the land, it's you. When you Pay Attention using this sense, you can also ask, "Where can I find _____?"

⊞ SENSE OF OTHERS

You know every rabbit that lives in the warren and even a few who don't. When you Pay Attention using this sense, you can also ask, "Who would know about _____?"

⊞ SQUIRMY

When you are smaller than what holds you, roll+Swift instead of +Strong when you Struggle.

⊞ STORYTELLER

When you tell a tale of your past exploits or about one or more of the Storied Characters, roll+Shrewd. On a 10+, reduce the Panic scores of your listeners by 3. On a 7-9, reduce their Panic scores by 1.

Storied Characters

There are stories that are bigger than any one warren, stories that are told everywhere rabbits live. The details change but these storied characters endure in the myths of rabbits.

- Moon Rabbit
- First Man and First Woman
- The Dog and the Fox
- Old Crow and Scarecrow
- The Lost Warren
- The Brave Prince or Princess

⊞ SWIFT RUNNER

You have never met an animal you couldn't outrun. When you Bolt, treat a roll of 6- as a 7-9.

⊞ SWIFT WARNING

When you alert others to danger, they each take +1 forward when responding to it.

⊞ THUMPER

When you cuff, kick, or knock another rabbit about, you may roll +Strong instead of +Shrewd when you Speak Plainly.

⊞ TOOTH AND CLAW

When you put up a fight, roll+Strong. On a 10+, they take a scar if they don't flee. On a 7-9, you both take a scar if you don't flee.

⊞ WORRIER

When you talk about your worries with another rabbit, remove their Panic, adding it to your own.

APPENDIX 2:
A Note on Humans

Don't go into Mr. McGregor's garden:
your Father had an accident there;
he was put in a pie by Mrs. McGregor.

Beatrix Potter, *The Tale of Peter Rabbit*

Traditionally, humans have had a love/hate relationship with rabbits—they love to catch rabbits in their traps or crosshairs but hate to catch them among their crops. In some areas where rabbits are not native, like Australia, rabbits have been considered such a threat that every trick from traps and poison to fences and disease has been used to diminish their number.

Humans use domesticated rabbits in various capacities. Some rabbits are bred for their fur. Others are raised for their meat. Rabbits are also used in biomedical research. Fancy rabbits are bred for show while others are raised and trained to win agility competitions. Many more are simply born into domestication to live out their lives as pets. All of these circumstances are useful setting fodder for *The Warren*. Rabbits in your game might start out in captivity but with the opportunity for escape or they may be intentionally or unintentionally released by their keepers. Rabbits in your games may wish to recover rabbits from human enclosures or otherwise disrupt the status quo.

Humans wear many hats in *The Warren*. Sometimes humans will be threats, sometimes predators, and sometimes just NPCs. A farmer plowing his fields for harvest might be a threat, a farmer's wife with a rifle might be a predator, and their empathetic daughter might be an NPC.

APPENDIX 3:
A Bit about Hares and Pikas

You are the hare of whom the proverb goes, Whose valor plucks dead lions by the beard.

William Shakespeare

Rabbits are members of the order of lagomorphs, along with hares and their "cousins" the pikas. *The Warren* focuses on rabbits but, in a pinch, you could play a game focused on hares or pikas. Similarly, hares and pikas can make excellent additions to the rabbits' world, as either friends or enemies, alone or in groups.

Like rabbits, hares are known for their elongated ears and hind limbs. Hares are typically larger and faster than rabbits. While rabbits congregate in subterranean warrens, hares prefer shallow depressions called "scrapes."

Pikas, on the other hand, have shorter, rounded ears and their hind limbs are less exaggerated.

Rabbits, hares, and pikas are similar in appearance and often confused; however, they are different enough that they cannot interbreed.

If you're interested in changing things up and playing a hare, see the *World of Borealis Wood* playset by Adam Drew, available from the *Bully Pulpit Games website*.

Some Lists

Some Pastoral Places

- Stream or pond, tasting of good moist forage
- Tall grass, stiff against your flanks
- Shorn grass, smelling of the cutting machine
- Stone wall or ditch, with faint sounds of what lies beyond
- Large rock or lone tree, with the mingled smells
  of all who have passed it
- Road or train tracks, a place cursed with the odor of death

Some Farmyard Places

- Parked trucks, tractors, and equipment smelling of oil
- Farmhouse, full of people and their noises
- Barn or shed, tasting of hay and livestock
- Outhouse, stinking sharply of people… and rats
- Coops and hutches, smelling of fear and desperation
- The tall things—a windmill or silo, dominating the landscape

Some Underground Places

- In damp soil among stone and boulders, smelling
  deliciousness above
- In dry rocky soil, feeling sharp stones on your paws
- In sandy soil amidst a tangle of wires, tasting grit
- In gritty soil beneath a concrete slab, swallowing your panic
- In peaty soil surrounded by roots, smelling
  the tree and its occupants
- In frozen soil, following ancient tunnels,
  the air dead and soundless

Some Park Places

- Jogging trail
- Streets
- Gutters and drains
- Streams and bridges
- Fountains
- Sports field
- Street light
- Statue or memorial
- Parked cars
- Sidewalks
- Public restrooms

Some Human Places

- Backyard hutch
- Research laboratory
- Fur farm
- Meat farm
- Zoo exhibit
- Children's classroom
- Veterinary clinic
- Planes, trains, and automobiles

Some Mountain Places

- Tree line
- Scree field
- Ridgeline
- Escarpment
- Gorge
- Peak
- Overhang
- Shepherd's hut
- Waterfall

Some Storied Characters

- Moon Rabbit
- First Man and First Woman
- The Dog and the Fox
- Old Crow and Scarecrow
- The Lost Warren
- The Brave Prince or Princess

Some Unheard of Things

- Swimming or using a raft
- Systems of writing
- Carrying objects
- Fighting as a group, or fighting a predator
- Defeating a snare
- Chewing out of a burlap sack

Some More Unheard of Things

- Manipulating fire
- Opening a closed door or kicking open a latch
- Diverting the flow of water
- Planting and sprouting seeds
- Having a séance or dream walking
- Systems of writing or communicating with a human

Some Predators

NORTH AMERICAN PREDATORS AND DANGERS

- Weasel
- Raccoon
- Coyote
- Alligator
- Qupqugiaq (Can appear as a dead relative to lure you into water, or as a ferocious eight-legged polar bear)
- Machine (Of destructive, unknown purpose)

SOUTH AMERICAN PREDATORS AND DANGERS

- Chemical
- White-Winged Vampire Bat
- Cougar
- Mapinguari (Its smell can cause panic, it can crush entire warrens)
- Eagle
- Lucifer Titi (Grasping hands, hungry for your kits)

ASIAN PREDATORS AND DANGERS

- Dhole
- Macaque
- Owl
- Ghost (Who have you wronged?)
- Pit (Newly dug by people)
- Tibetan Fox

AUSTRALIAN PREDATORS AND DANGERS

- Dingo
- Poison (Set out for rabbits, and tempting)
- Crocodile
- Funnel Web Spider
- Bunyip (Stay away from its pond)
- Bandicoot (Brings disease)

AFRICAN PREDATORS AND DANGERS

- Paw Trap (For servals; it will take your limb clean off)
- Banded Mongoose
- Nandi Bear (Hungry and relentless by night)
- Serval
- Snake
- Hyena

EUROPEAN PREDATORS AND DANGERS

- Badger
- Hawk
- Goblin (Wants to be King)
- Dog
- Snare (Set to catch and choke rabbits)
- Stoat

Some Predators, Ready to Go

Dog

Trait: Lazy, vacuous, or starchy

- Bark and bark and bark
- Give chase
- Bite and shake
- Sniff out a trail
- Widen an existing hole

Fox

Trait: Sly, desperate, or merely curious

- Disappear and reappear
- Bite and hold
- Follow at a distance
- Entice and make assurances
- Hold a grudge

Hawk

Trait: Shrewd, merciless, or sated

- Swoop from above
- Gouge with talons
- Rend with beak
- Snatch and carry away
- Buffet with wings

Hunters

Trait: Drunk, youthful, or persistent

- Fire their guns
- Use spotlights
- Search out the warren
- Plug escape tunnels
- Set traps and snares
- Loose dogs

Snares

Trait: Cage, hoop, or jawed

- Hold them in place
- Inflict pain
- Starve or dehydrate
- Leave them exposed
- Allow for their capture

Some Threats, Ready to Go

The Threat of the Highway

Intent: To snake across the land
- Men arrive to survey the land
- Machines ravage the pasture
- Trucks leave piles of dirt and gravel
- The land is bisected

The Threat of Kudzu

Intent: To envelop the grove
- Leaves blot out the sun
- Nest of predators
- Deadfall trees fall
- Humans spray toxic chemicals

The Threat of Harvest

Intent: To strip the fields
- Humans everywhere
- Deafening noise
- Bald patches of land
- Machines shake the ground

The Threat of Cottontail's Ascendancy

Intent: To reorder the warren's hierarchy
- Some rabbits are cagey
- Cottontail's followers barricade tunnels
- Cottontail's followers exile Major Ears
- Cottontail assigns new social statuses

The Threat of Spring Showers

Intent: To become Summer

- Thorns grow thick
- Cacophony of baby birds
- Torrential rains
- Grass grows tall

The Threat of Blazing Summer

Intent: To become Fall

- The day goes on and on
- Thick, thick vegetation
- Pastoral views attract humans
- Water sources run dry

The Threat of Late Fall

Intent: To become Winter

- Leaves change color and fall
- Harvest brings humans
- Fields lie fallow and empty
- The birds depart

The Threat of Biting Winter

Intent: To become Spring

- Cold, cold nights
- Snow blankets the ground
- Food becomes scarce
- Hunters hunt

The Threat of Haystack Warren

Intent: To annex the warren

- Emissaries arrive from Haystack Warren
- Soldiers amass on the border
- Access to the stream is cut off
- Burrowers breach the warren

The X-Card

by John Stavropoulos

The X-Card is a useful technique, developed to help make games safer and more inclusive. Literally an index card with an X on it, the card can be used to edit out anything that makes a player uncomfortable with no explanations needed. To use the X-Card, say the following at the beginning of play:

"I'd like your help to make this game fun for everyone.

"If anything in the game makes anyone uncomfortable...
[draw an X on an index card]

"...just lift this card up, or simply tap it.

"You don't have to explain why—it doesn't matter why.

"When anyone lifts or taps this card, we'll simply edit out the fictional details being X-Carded.

"And if there is ever an issue, anyone can call for a break and we can talk privately.

"I know it sounds funny but it will help us play amazing games together...

"...and usually I'm the one who uses the X-Card to protect myself from all of you!"

For a thorough breakdown of the technique: *tinyurl.com/x-card-rpg*

APPENDIX 6:
Mediography

Roleplaying Games

Apocalypse World, D. Vincent Baker

Dungeon World, Sage Latorra and Adam Koebel

Simple World, Avery Mcdaldno

Bunnies & Burrows, B. Dennis Sustare and Scott Robinson

Bunnies & Burrows (GURPS), Steffan O'Sullivan

Rabbit Fiction

Watership Down*, Richard Adams

Tales from Watership Down, Richard Adams

Fifteen Rabbits, Felix Salten

Bambi, a Life in the Woods*, Felix Salten

Bambi's Children, Felix Salten

The Warren, Fred L. Tate

Rabbit Hill, Robert Lawson

The Tough Winter, Robert Lawson

The Abominable Charles Christopher, Karl Kerschl

The Animals of Farthing Wood*, Colin Dann

Tales of Uncle Remus, Joel Chandler Harris

Robbut: A Tale of Tails*, Robert Lawson

Swamper: Letters from a Louisiana Swamp Rabbit, Amy Griffen Ouchley

Animal Lives: Rabbits, Sally Tagholm

Rabbit Non-Fiction

Rabbits: The Animal Answer Guide, Susan Lumpkin and John Seidenstickerz

Stories Rabbits Tell: A Natural and Cultural History of a Misunderstood Creature, Susan E. Davis and Margo Demello

The Private Life of the Rabbit, Ronald Lockley

Domestic Rabbits and Their Histories: Breeds of the World, Bob D. Whitman

In Pursuit of Coney, David Brian Plummer

Rabbit Storybooks

Peter Rabbit, Beatrix Potter

Benjamin Bunny, Beatrix Potter

The Tale of the Flopsy Bunnies, Beatrix Potter

The Rabbits, John Marsden

The Rabbit's Wedding, Garth Williams

Rabbits and Raindrops, Jim Arnosky

*Denotes an animated version also

Glossary

2d6: A notation that stands for two 6-sided dice.

Advance: A new move gained by a PC once during each chapter.

Agenda: A GM's goal in play.

Buck: A male rabbit.

Burrow: An individual rabbit's underground place to sleep and birth litters in a larger warren.

Chapter: A unit of play with a clear narrative arc, usually about a session long.

Doe: A female rabbit.

Fiction: All the imaginary details of the game.

GM: The person who controls everything else in the game.

GM Move: A specific event introduced by the GM as the result of a player's actions or a move. Can be a soft or hard move.

Kit or Kitten: A baby rabbit.

Litter: All the rabbits born of one pregnancy.

Move: A rule that determines the outcome of a specific event in the fiction.

Non-Player Character (NPC): A rabbit, animal, or person controlled by the GM.

Panic: A PC stat that measures stress taken by the rabbit.

Player: A person who controls a rabbit character in the game.

Player Character (PC): A rabbit controlled by a player.

Player Move: A specific move introduced by the player. Can be a Basic, Special, or Character move.

Predator: An animal that preys on rabbits in one way or another, including humans and even other rabbits.

Principle: A guideline for the GM.

Retirement: Removing a PC from the story, either through death or by making them an NPC.

Roll: Roll 2d6 and sum their results.

Scar: Harm taken by a PC that makes a move unavailable.

Session: A unit of real-world play, a sitting.

Threat: A dynamic aspect of the game's setting.

Warren: A tangle of tunnels and burrows where rabbits live.

Name

....

Barley, Lily, Honey, Holly, Pumpkin, Thorn, Dusty, Midnight, Patches, Poppy, Snow, Bine, Floppy, Basil, Misty, Nutmeg, Breeze, Dewdrop, Charcoal, Sandy, Truffle, Olive, Ash, Chestnut, Ivy, Meadow

portrait
draw your rabbit

Looks

Circle one from each category

Body: Lean, stocky, compact, long, frail, sick, runt;

Coat: Lush, Sleek, Distinctive, Unusual Color, Mangy, Singed

Ears: Long, Short, Floppy, Tattered, ID-Tagged, Just the One

Parts: Buck, Doe (☐ Pregnant)

Stats

Assign one to each stat: +2, +1, 0, -1.

strong	swift	steady
shrewd	max panic	current
	5 +/- Steady	Starts at 0

the warren

www.bullypulpitgames.com/warren

Basic Moves

⊞ RESIST PANIC

When you expose yourself to new dangers, roll+Steady. On a 10+, you're unshaken. On a 7-9, you manage to keep it together but take +1 Panic. On a miss, take +1 Panic as you cower, hesitate, or flee—the GM can offer you a worse outcome, a hard bargain, or an ugly choice.

⊞ SPEAK PLAINLY

When you reason with another animal, roll+Shrewd. On a 10+, NPCs will do as you ask given the proper assurances. On a 7-9, they do as you ask provided you meet one of their demands now.

⊞ PAY ATTENTION

When you give your full attention, roll+Shrewd. On a 10+, hold 2. On a 7-9, hold 1. On a 6-, hold 1 but you open yourself up to danger. Holds may be spent, 1 for 1, to name a sense and ask the GM one of the questions below. The GM will tell you what your sense reveals; take +1 forward when acting on the answers.

- What here is the greatest danger to me?
- What will happen if I stay very still?
- Where can I flee to?
- Are they telling the truth?
- What do they wish I'd do?
- How could I get _____?

⊞ BOLT

When you make a run for it, roll+Swift. On a 10+, you run like the wind. On a 7-9, you run fast enough but choose one:

- You don't end up exactly where you intended.
- It takes more out of you than you would have thought, take -1 forward.
- It's much closer than you care for, take +1 Panic.

⊞ SNEAK

When you take pains to avoid notice, roll+Shrewd. On a 10+, pick three. On a 7-9, pick one:

- Behind cover
- Silent
- Downwind
- No tracks

⊞ HELP/HINDER

When you help or hinder another player character's rabbit, roll and add whichever stat the GM deems appropriate. On a 10+, give +1 or -1 to that player's roll or Panic. On a 7-9 do the same, but your fate is tied to theirs.

Character Moves

....
....
....
....
....
....
....
....
....
....
....
....
....
....
....
....
....
....
....
....
....
....
....
....
....
....
....
....
....
....
....
....
....

Special Moves

RELAX

When you play, groom, or rest in relative safety, subtract 1 from your Panic.

STRUGGLE

When you struggle to free yourself, roll+Strong. You may then take Panic, 1 for 1, to increase your roll. On a 10+ you manage to wriggle free. On a 7-9, you can wriggle free if you are willing to take a scar. On a 6-, you can't escape and you take a scar anyway.

COMPETE

When you compete with another PC rabbit, both of you choose a value on a die and then reveal it. If one rabbit's die shows a higher face, they get their way and choose a value from one of the dice—both of you take that much Panic. If neither is higher, no one gets their way and you both take Panic equal to the dice value.

DIG

When you dig in the earth, roll+Strong. On a 10+, you scratch out a simple burrow or otherwise quickly shift some dirt. On a 7-9, choose one:

- You can only dig enough space to squeeze yourself into.
- Your excavation is unstable and temporary at best.
- You take significantly longer than expected.

MATE

When you mate with another rabbit, take +1 ongoing to Help/Hinder that rabbit until you mate with someone else. If you are different genders, both of you hide zero or one die in your fist. On the count of three, open your hands—two dice means the doe is pregnant and she may give birth whenever it feels right.

BIRTH A LITTER

When you Birth a Litter, roll and subtract your current Panic to determine the number of kits that are born. On a 10+, it's an unusually sizable litter—increase your Panic to maximum. On a 7-9, a normal-sized litter is by no means easy—take +2 Panic. On a 6-, it's all just too much and few if any survive. The GM still gets to make a hard move but this is a good time to check in and make sure other players are comfortable with the fiction.

INNOVATE

When you do something unheard of, imagine what your actions would look like as a move. Say what triggers the move and roll. On a 7+, work with the GM to write the move—it is now a Special move for the remainder of the game and your roll stands. On a miss, it's not something rabbits can ever do and there will certainly be consequences.

TIME GOES BY

When months or seasons pass, roll the dice. As a group, decide which die represents births and which represents deaths. Add rabbits to the warren according to the birth die and subtract rabbits from the warren according to the death die.

RETIRE

When you give up the ghost or the spotlight, hold 1 and describe how your rabbit retires from play, then make a new rabbit. The hold may be spent to give any rabbit an additional Character move.

Advancement

During play, each PC may take one additional Character move each chapter as they learn, grow, or change. The move cannot be one already claimed by another character.

When you claim this move, mark it on your rabbit playbook. If you haven't claimed it by the end of the chapter, do it at that time.

Notes

....
....
....
....
....
....
....
....
....
....
....
....
....

Name

....

Jack, Parsley, Foxglove, Cutter, Lightning, Rose, Gale, Dandelion, Tin, Willow, Straw, Cotton, Thyme, Wind, Sunshine, Rainstorm, Peanut, Swiftpaw, Windrunner, Nibble, Digger, Squeek, Raincatcher, Blackberry, Coriander

portrait
draw your rabbit

Looks

Circle one from each category

Body: Lean, stocky, compact, long, frail, sick, runt;

Coat: Lush, Sleek, Distinctive, Unusual Color, Mangy, Singed

Ears: Long, Short, Floppy, Tattered, ID-Tagged, Just the One

Parts: Buck, Doe (☐ Pregnant)

Stats

Assign one to each stat: +2, +1, 0, -1.

strong	swift	steady
shrewd	max panic	current
	5 +/- Steady	Starts at 0

the warren

www.bullypulpitgames.com/warren

Basic Moves

▦ RESIST PANIC

When you expose yourself to new dangers, roll+Steady. On a 10+, you're unshaken. On a 7-9, you manage to keep it together but take +1 Panic. On a miss, take +1 Panic as you cower, hesitate, or flee—the GM can offer you a worse outcome, a hard bargain, or an ugly choice.

▦ SPEAK PLAINLY

When you reason with another animal, roll+Shrewd. On a 10+, NPCs will do as you ask given the proper assurances. On a 7-9, they do as you ask provided you meet one of their demands now.

▦ PAY ATTENTION

When you give your full attention, roll+Shrewd. On a 10+, hold 2. On a 7-9, hold 1. On a 6-, hold 1 but you open yourself up to danger. Holds may be spent, 1 for 1, to name a sense and ask the GM one of the questions below. The GM will tell you what your sense reveals; take +1 forward when acting on the answers.

- What here is the greatest danger to me?
- What will happen if I stay very still?
- Where can I flee to?
- Are they telling the truth?
- What do they wish I'd do?
- How could I get _____?

▦ BOLT

When you make a run for it, roll+Swift. On a 10+, you run like the wind. On a 7-9, you run fast enough but choose one:

- You don't end up exactly where you intended.
- It takes more out of you than you would have thought, take -1 forward.
- It's much closer than you care for, take +1 Panic.

▦ SNEAK

When you take pains to avoid notice, roll+Shrewd. On a 10+, pick three. On a 7-9, pick one:

- Behind cover
- Silent
- Downwind
- No tracks

▦ HELP/HINDER

When you help or hinder another player character's rabbit, roll and add whichever stat the GM deems appropriate. On a 10+, give +1 or -1 to that player's roll or Panic. On a 7-9 do the same, but your fate is tied to theirs.

Character Moves

....

....

....

....

....

....

....

....

....

....

....

....

....

....

....

....

....

....

....

....

....

....

....

....

....

....

....

....

....

....

....

Special Moves

RELAX

When you play, groom, or rest in relative safety, subtract 1 from your Panic.

STRUGGLE

When you struggle to free yourself, roll+Strong. You may then take Panic, 1 for 1, to increase your roll. On a 10+ you manage to wriggle free. On a 7-9, you can wriggle free if you are willing to take a scar. On a 6-, you can't escape and you take a scar anyway.

COMPETE

When you compete with another PC rabbit, both of you choose a value on a die and then reveal it. If one rabbit's die shows a higher face, they get their way and choose a value from one of the dice—both of you take that much Panic. If neither is higher, no one gets their way and you both take Panic equal to the dice value.

DIG

When you dig in the earth, roll+Strong. On a 10+, you scratch out a simple burrow or otherwise quickly shift some dirt. On a 7-9, choose one:

- You can only dig enough space to squeeze yourself into.
- Your excavation is unstable and temporary at best.
- You take significantly longer than expected.

MATE

When you mate with another rabbit, take +1 ongoing to Help/Hinder that rabbit until you mate with someone else. If you are different genders, both of you hide zero or one die in your fist. On the count of three, open your hands—two dice means the doe is pregnant and she may give birth whenever it feels right.

BIRTH A LITTER

When you Birth a Litter, roll and subtract your current Panic to determine the number of kits that are born. On a 10+, it's an unusually sizable litter—increase your Panic to maximum. On a 7-9, a normal-sized litter is by no means easy—take +2 Panic. On a 6-, it's all just too much and few if any survive. The GM still gets to make a hard move but this is a good time to check in and make sure other players are comfortable with the fiction.

INNOVATE

When you do something unheard of, imagine what your actions would look like as a move. Say what triggers the move and roll. On a 7+, work with the GM to write the move—it is now a Special move for the remainder of the game and your roll stands. On a miss, it's not something rabbits can ever do and there will certainly be consequences.

TIME GOES BY

When months or seasons pass, roll the dice. As a group, decide which die represents births and which represents deaths. Add rabbits to the warren according to the birth die and subtract rabbits from the warren according to the death die.

RETIRE

When you give up the ghost or the spotlight, hold 1 and describe how your rabbit retires from play, then make a new rabbit. The hold may be spent to give any rabbit an additional Character move.

Advancement

During play, each PC may take one additional Character move each chapter as they learn, grow, or change. The move cannot be one already claimed by another character.

When you claim this move, mark it on your rabbit playbook. If you haven't claimed it by the end of the chapter, do it at that time.

Notes

....
....
....
....
....
....
....
....
....
....
....
....
....

Name

....

Milkweed, Cress, Lineberry, Button, Grooveburr, Mulberry, Dewberry, Pansy, Marigold, , Blackthorn, Holly, Ivy, Dogwood, Honeysuckle, Buttercup, Snowflake, Sorrel, Bracken, Poppy, Sundew, Birch, Adler, Bounder

portrait
draw your rabbit

Looks

Circle one from each category

Body: Lean, stocky, compact, long, frail, sick, runt;

Coat: Lush, Sleek, Distinctive, Unusual Color, Mangy, Singed

Ears: Long, Short, Floppy, Tattered, ID-Tagged, Just the One

Parts: Buck, Doe (☐ Pregnant)

Stats

Assign one to each stat: +2, +1, 0, -1.

strong	swift	steady
shrewd	max panic	current
	5 +/- Steady	Starts at 0

the warren

Basic Moves

▦ RESIST PANIC

When you expose yourself to new dangers, roll+Steady. On a 10+, you're unshaken. On a 7-9, you manage to keep it together but take +1 Panic. On a miss, take +1 Panic as you cower, hesitate, or flee—the GM can offer you a worse outcome, a hard bargain, or an ugly choice.

▦ SPEAK PLAINLY

When you reason with another animal, roll+Shrewd. On a 10+, NPCs will do as you ask given the proper assurances. On a 7-9, they do as you ask provided you meet one of their demands now.

▦ PAY ATTENTION

When you give your full attention, roll+Shrewd. On a 10+, hold 2. On a 7-9, hold 1. On a 6-, hold 1 but you open yourself up to danger. Holds may be spent, 1 for 1, to name a sense and ask the GM one of the questions below. The GM will tell you what your sense reveals; take +1 forward when acting on the answers.

- What here is the greatest danger to me?
- What will happen if I stay very still?
- Where can I flee to?
- Are they telling the truth?
- What do they wish I'd do?
- How could I get _____?

▦ BOLT

When you make a run for it, roll+Swift. On a 10+, you run like the wind. On a 7-9, you run fast enough but choose one:

- You don't end up exactly where you intended.
- It takes more out of you than you would have thought, take -1 forward.
- It's much closer than you care for, take +1 Panic.

▦ SNEAK

When you take pains to avoid notice, roll+Shrewd. On a 10+, pick three. On a 7-9, pick one:

- Behind cover
- Silent
- Downwind
- No tracks

▦ HELP/HINDER

When you help or hinder another player character's rabbit, roll and add whichever stat the GM deems appropriate. On a 10+, give +1 or -1 to that player's roll or Panic. On a 7-9 do the same, but your fate is tied to theirs.

Character Moves

....
....
....
....
....
....
....
....
....
....
....
....
....
....
....
....
....
....
....
....
....
....
....
....
....
....
....
....
....
....
....
....
....
....
....
....
....

Special Moves

⊞ RELAX

When you play, groom, or rest in relative safety, subtract 1 from your Panic.

⊞ STRUGGLE

When you struggle to free yourself, roll+Strong. You may then take Panic, 1 for 1, to increase your roll. On a 10+ you manage to wriggle free. On a 7-9, you can wriggle free if you are willing to take a scar. On a 6-, you can't escape and you take a scar anyway.

⊞ COMPETE

When you compete with another PC rabbit, both of you choose a value on a die and then reveal it. If one rabbit's die shows a higher face, they get their way and choose a value from one of the dice—both of you take that much Panic. If neither is higher, no one gets their way and you both take Panic equal to the dice value.

⊞ DIG

When you dig in the earth, roll+Strong. On a 10+, you scratch out a simple burrow or otherwise quickly shift some dirt. On a 7-9, choose one:

- You can only dig enough space to squeeze yourself into.
- Your excavation is unstable and temporary at best.
- You take significantly longer than expected.

⊞ MATE

When you mate with another rabbit, take +1 ongoing to Help/Hinder that rabbit until you mate with someone else. If you are different genders, both of you hide zero or one die in your fist. On the count of three, open your hands—two dice means the doe is pregnant and she may give birth whenever it feels right.

⊞ BIRTH A LITTER

When you Birth a Litter, roll and subtract your current Panic to determine the number of kits that are born. On a 10+, it's an unusually sizable litter—increase your Panic to maximum. On a 7-9, a normal-sized litter is by no means easy—take +2 Panic. On a 6-, it's all just too much and few if any survive. The GM still gets to make a hard move but this is a good time to check in and make sure other players are comfortable with the fiction.

⊞ INNOVATE

When you do something unheard of, imagine what your actions would look like as a move. Say what triggers the move and roll. On a 7+, work with the GM to write the move—it is now a Special move for the remainder of the game and your roll stands. On a miss, it's not something rabbits can ever do and there will certainly be consequences.

⊞ TIME GOES BY

When months or seasons pass, roll the dice. As a group, decide which die represents births and which represents deaths. Add rabbits to the warren according to the birth die and subtract rabbits from the warren according to the death die.

⊞ RETIRE

When you give up the ghost or the spotlight, hold 1 and describe how your rabbit retires from play, then make a new rabbit. The hold may be spent to give any rabbit an additional Character move.

Advancement

During play, each PC may take one additional Character move each chapter as they learn, grow, or change. The move cannot be one already claimed by another character.

When you claim this move, mark it on your rabbit playbook. If you haven't claimed it by the end of the chapter, do it at that time.

Notes

....
....
....
....
....
....
....
....
....
....
....
....
....

Name

....

Rosemary, Aster, Thistle, Sedge, Cress, Boxwood, Heath, Snowflake, Foxglove, Primrose, Yarrow, Columbine, Heartleaf, Moonbeam, Dahlia, Woodruff, Hellebore, Lily, Iris, Nettle, Spot, Hyacinth, Moss, Verbena, Tulip, Juniper

portrait
draw your rabbit

Looks

Circle one from each category

Body: Lean, stocky, compact, long, frail, sick, runt;

Coat: Lush, Sleek, Distinctive, Unusual Color, Mangy, Singed

Ears: Long, Short, Floppy, Tattered, ID-Tagged, Just the One

Parts: Buck, Doe (□ Pregnant)

Stats

Assign one to each stat: +2, +1, 0, -1.

strong	swift	steady
shrewd	max panic	current
	5 +/- Steady	Starts at 0

the warren

www.bullypulpitgames.com/warren

Basic Moves

⊞ RESIST PANIC

When you expose yourself to new dangers, roll+Steady. On a 10+, you're unshaken. On a 7-9, you manage to keep it together but take +1 Panic. On a miss, take +1 Panic as you cower, hesitate, or flee—the GM can offer you a worse outcome, a hard bargain, or an ugly choice.

⊞ SPEAK PLAINLY

When you reason with another animal, roll+Shrewd. On a 10+, NPCs will do as you ask given the proper assurances. On a 7-9, they do as you ask provided you meet one of their demands now.

⊞ PAY ATTENTION

When you give your full attention, roll+Shrewd. On a 10+, hold 2. On a 7-9, hold 1. On a 6-, hold 1 but you open yourself up to danger. Holds may be spent, 1 for 1, to name a sense and ask the GM one of the questions below. The GM will tell you what your sense reveals; take +1 forward when acting on the answers.

- What here is the greatest danger to me?
- What will happen if I stay very still?
- Where can I flee to?
- Are they telling the truth?
- What do they wish I'd do?
- How could I get _____?

⊞ BOLT

When you make a run for it, roll+Swift. On a 10+, you run like the wind. On a 7-9, you run fast enough but choose one:

- You don't end up exactly where you intended.
- It takes more out of you than you would have thought, take -1 forward.
- It's much closer than you care for, take +1 Panic.

⊞ SNEAK

When you take pains to avoid notice, roll+Shrewd. On a 10+, pick three. On a 7-9, pick one:

- Behind cover
- Silent
- Downwind
- No tracks

⊞ HELP/HINDER

When you help or hinder another player character's rabbit, roll and add whichever stat the GM deems appropriate. On a 10+, give +1 or -1 to that player's roll or Panic. On a 7-9 do the same, but your fate is tied to theirs.

Character Moves

....
....
....
....
....
....
....
....
....
....
....
....
....
....
....
....
....
....
....
....
....
....
....
....
....
....
....
....
....
....
....
....
....
....
....
....
....
....

Special Moves

RELAX

When you play, groom, or rest in relative safety, subtract 1 from your Panic.

STRUGGLE

When you struggle to free yourself, roll+Strong. You may then take Panic, 1 for 1, to increase your roll. On a 10+ you manage to wriggle free. On a 7-9, you can wriggle free if you are willing to take a scar. On a 6-, you can't escape and you take a scar anyway.

COMPETE

When you compete with another PC rabbit, both of you choose a value on a die and then reveal it. If one rabbit's die shows a higher face, they get their way and choose a value from one of the dice—both of you take that much Panic. If neither is higher, no one gets their way and you both take Panic equal to the dice value.

DIG

When you dig in the earth, roll+Strong. On a 10+, you scratch out a simple burrow or otherwise quickly shift some dirt. On a 7-9, choose one:

- You can only dig enough space to squeeze yourself into.
- Your excavation is unstable and temporary at best.
- You take significantly longer than expected.

MATE

When you mate with another rabbit, take +1 ongoing to Help/Hinder that rabbit until you mate with someone else. If you are different genders, both of you hide zero or one die in your fist. On the count of three, open your hands—two dice means the doe is pregnant and she may give birth whenever it feels right.

BIRTH A LITTER

When you Birth a Litter, roll and subtract your current Panic to determine the number of kits that are born. On a 10+, it's an unusually sizable litter—increase your Panic to maximum. On a 7-9, a normal-sized litter is by no means easy—take +2 Panic. On a 6-, it's all just too much and few if any survive. The GM still gets to make a hard move but this is a good time to check in and make sure other players are comfortable with the fiction.

INNOVATE

When you do something unheard of, imagine what your actions would look like as a move. Say what triggers the move and roll. On a 7+, work with the GM to write the move—it is now a Special move for the remainder of the game and your roll stands. On a miss, it's not something rabbits can ever do and there will certainly be consequences.

TIME GOES BY

When months or seasons pass, roll the dice. As a group, decide which die represents births and which represents deaths. Add rabbits to the warren according to the birth die and subtract rabbits from the warren according to the death die.

RETIRE

When you give up the ghost or the spotlight, hold 1 and describe how your rabbit retires from play, then make a new rabbit. The hold may be spent to give any rabbit an additional Character move.

Advancement

During play, each PC may take one additional Character move each chapter as they learn, grow, or change. The move cannot be one already claimed by another character.

When you claim this move, mark it on your rabbit playbook. If you haven't claimed it by the end of the chapter, do it at that time.

Notes

....
....
....
....
....
....
....
....
....
....
....
....
....

Name

....

Jack, Parsley, Foxglove, Cutter, Lightning, Rose, Gale, Dandelion, Tin, Willow, Straw, Cotton, Thyme, Wind, Sunshine, Rainstorm, Peanut, Swiftpaw, Windrunner, Nibble, Digger, Squeek, Raincatcher, Blackberry, Coriander

portrait
draw your rabbit

Looks

Circle one from each category

Body: Lean, stocky, compact, long, frail, sick, runt;

Coat: Lush, Sleek, Distinctive, Unusual Color, Mangy, Singed

Ears: Long, Short, Floppy, Tattered, ID-Tagged, Just the One

Parts: Buck, Doe (☐ Pregnant)

Stats

Assign one to each stat: +2, +1, 0, -1.

strong	swift	steady
shrewd	max panic	current
	5 +/- Steady	Starts at 0

the warren

www.bullypulpitgames.com/warren

Basic Moves

⊞ RESIST PANIC

When you expose yourself to new dangers, roll+Steady. On a 10+, you're unshaken. On a 7-9, you manage to keep it together but take +1 Panic. On a miss, take +1 Panic as you cower, hesitate, or flee—the GM can offer you a worse outcome, a hard bargain, or an ugly choice.

⊞ SPEAK PLAINLY

When you reason with another animal, roll+Shrewd. On a 10+, NPCs will do as you ask given the proper assurances. On a 7-9, they do as you ask provided you meet one of their demands now.

⊞ PAY ATTENTION

When you give your full attention, roll+Shrewd. On a 10+, hold 2. On a 7-9, hold 1. On a 6-, hold 1 but you open yourself up to danger. Holds may be spent, 1 for 1, to name a sense and ask the GM one of the questions below. The GM will tell you what your sense reveals; take +1 forward when acting on the answers.

- What here is the greatest danger to me?
- What will happen if I stay very still?
- Where can I flee to?
- Are they telling the truth?
- What do they wish I'd do?
- How could I get _____?

⊞ BOLT

When you make a run for it, roll+Swift. On a 10+, you run like the wind. On a 7-9, you run fast enough but choose one:

- You don't end up exactly where you intended.
- It takes more out of you than you would have thought, take -1 forward.
- It's much closer than you care for, take +1 Panic.

⊞ SNEAK

When you take pains to avoid notice, roll+Shrewd. On a 10+, pick three. On a 7-9, pick one:

- Behind cover
- Silent
- Downwind
- No tracks

⊞ HELP/HINDER

When you help or hinder another player character's rabbit, roll and add whichever stat the GM deems appropriate. On a 10+, give +1 or -1 to that player's roll or Panic. On a 7-9 do the same, but your fate is tied to theirs.

Character Moves

....
....
....
....
....
....
....
....
....
....
....
....
....
....
....
....
....
....
....
....
....
....
....
....
....
....
....
....
....
....
....
....
....
....
....
....
....

Special Moves (Kids)

⊞ RELAX

When you play, groom, or rest in relative safety, subtract 1 from your Panic.

⊞ STRUGGLE

When you struggle to free yourself, roll+Strong. You may then take Panic, 1 for 1, to increase your roll. On a 10+ you manage to wriggle free. On a 7-9, you can wriggle free if you are willing to take a scar. On a 6-, you can't escape and you take a scar anyway.

⊞ COMPETE

When you compete with another PC rabbit, both of you choose a value on a die and then reveal it. If one rabbit's die shows a higher face, they get their way and choose a value from one of the dice—both of you take that much Panic. If neither is higher, no one gets their way and you both take Panic equal to the dice value.

⊞ DIG

When you dig in the earth, roll+Strong. On a 10+, you scratch out a simple burrow or otherwise quickly shift some dirt. On a 7-9, choose one:

- You can only dig enough space to squeeze yourself into.
- Your excavation is unstable and temporary at best.
- You take significantly longer than expected.

⊞ BEST FRIEND

When you have a best friend, tell them so and take +1 ongoing to Help/Hinder that rabbit until you decide to be best friends with someone else.

⊞ LITTERMATE

When you are born to the same litter, share your earliest memories and take +1 ongoing to Help/Hinder that rabbit until another relationship becomes more important.

⊞ BIRTH A LITTER

When you Birth a Litter, roll and subtract your current Panic to determine the number of kits that are born. On a 10+, it's an unusually sizable litter—increase your Panic to maximum. On a 7-9, a normal-sized litter is by no means easy—take +2 Panic. On a 6-, it's all just too much and few if any survive. The GM still gets to make a hard move but this is a good time to check in and make sure other players are comfortable with the fiction.

⊞ INNOVATE

When you do something unheard of, imagine what your actions would look like as a move. Say what triggers the move and roll. On a 7+, work with the GM to write the move—it is now a Special move for the remainder of the game and your roll stands. On a miss, it's not something rabbits can ever do and there will certainly be consequences.

⊞ TIME GOES BY

When months or seasons pass, roll the dice. As a group, decide which die represents births and which represents deaths. Add rabbits to the warren according to the birth die and subtract rabbits from the warren according to the death die.

⊞ RETIRE

When you give up the ghost or the spotlight, hold 1 and describe how your rabbit retires from play, then make a new rabbit. The hold may be spent to give any rabbit an additional Character move.

Advancement

During play, each PC may take one additional Character move each chapter as they learn, grow, or change. The move cannot be one already claimed by another character.

When you claim this move, mark it on your rabbit playbook. If you haven't claimed it by the end of the chapter, do it at that time.

Notes

....
....
....
....
....
....
....
....
....
....
....
....
....
....

Additional Thanks

This game would not be what it is without the support of our Kickstarter backers. We owe a special thanks to the following people for their generous support and enthusiasm.

The Black Rabbit

Paul Alexander Butler

Explorers

Robert Biskin, Patrick Leonard, Carl Rigney, John Waclawski, and Lester Ward

Tricksters

Stephen Allen, Brian Allred, Simon Andersson, Will Andrews, Steve Angel, Courtney Apgar, Mark Argent, Tresi Arvizo, Oliver Ashour, Peter Augerot, Shaun Bailey, Vincent Baker, Joseph Bargerhuff, Kerri Barnes, Thomas Baxter, Joe Beason, Chris Bekofske, Iacopo Benigni, Russell Benner, Travis Bentz, Simon Berman, Paul "Yub Yub" Blair, Heather Blandford, Matthew Blanski, Adam Blinkinsop, Brian Blundell, David Bourdon, Edward Bourelle, Matthew Bourjaily, Kim Brandes, Patrick Brannick, Nate Brengle, Peter R Brooks, Christopher G. Brown, Ryan Michael Brown, Jordan Brummond, Simon Brunning, Darren Buckley, Brian Burke, Steve Burnett, Wolfie BW, Kevin Caldwell, Hamish Cameron, Twyla Campbell, Robert Carnel, Damian Caruana, David Castillo, Dan Cetorelli, Caroline Choong, Beth Chow, Leen Claes, Jason Cleveland, Lillian Cohen- Moore, Angela Collins, Derrick Cook, Jesse Coombs, Christopher Corbett, Jason Cordova, Alec Coxe, Tucker Craig, Marc Cram, Tyson Cram, Stephen Crawford, Yoshi Creelman, Jeff Crews, Walter F. Croft, Josh Crowe, CryAxe, George Cummings, Brodie Dayton-Mills, Govert de Jongh, Karl

Deckard, Mark Delsing, James Deming, Joe Depeau, Howard Des Chenes, Chip Dickerson, Jeff Dieterle, Maria DiFuccia, Phill Donaldson, Steve Donohue, Adam Drew, Sean Duncan, Herman Duyker, Paul Echeverri, Christer Edling, Mary Emme, Måns Ericsson, Simon Etwell, Mark Ferguson, Andrew Fish, Jessica Fishstein, and Big Wig Fiver, Raymond Flaig, Shauna Forrister, Sir Walter Freckleton, Jeremy Friesen, Kristoffer From, Jennifer Fuss, The Fuzziest Kitty, Matthew Gagan, Ed Gallagher, David Gallo, Skyhaven Games, Dusdan Garver, Lorenzo Gatti, Paul Gillibrand, Max Glasner, Keith Goken, Thiago Gonçalves, Vel Grande, Richard Greene, Schubacca *growl*, Derek Guder, Jack Gulick, Andrew Hackard, Ara Hacopian, Lisa Haglund, Hakan & Kate, Dan Hall, Justin Hamilton, Adam Harrison, Nathan Herrold, Amelia Hite and Family, Frost Holliman, John "The Fog" Holt, Nick Hopkins, Nathan Howell, Ambur Hsiao, James Hudyma, Christine Hung, Lucy Hunley, Lance Hurst, Jeffrey James, Tim Jensen, Colin Jessup, Jasen Johns, Erik Johnson, Thomas Johnston, Corwin Juras, Toshihiko Kambayashi, Robin Keijser, Sungil Kim, Paul Mitchell Kip, Jeffrey Kirby, Sabrina Klevenow, Doug Kovacs, Michael Kruckvich, Robert Kukuchka, Ivan Kvapil, Zack Latham, Sage LaTorra, Christopher Lauricella, Christopher Leaton, Socvun Dollar Lee, Adam Lee, Petri Leinonen, Luca Lettieri, Bowah Leung, Sean Leventhal, Daniel Lewis, Daniel Ley, Cameron Little, Ryan and Rebecca Lohmeyer, Frank Lopez, Ryan Lowy, Kurt Loy, Jason Lutes, Ryan Macklin, Rhodrick Magsino, Marc Majcher, Lasse Malinen, Claire Malley, Nich Maragos, John Marron, Sam May, John B. McCarthy, Claire McCarthy, Jonathan McCulley, Chris McEligot, Ian McFarlin, Tucker McKinnon, Dennis McNicholas, Miles McPea, Ed McW, John Mehrholz, James Mendez Hodes, Trey Mercer, Ryan Mererdith, Eric Mersmann, Brandon Metcalf, Gray Miller, David Millians, Andrew Montgomery-Hurrell, Clinton Morris,

Flavio Mortarino, Conrad Motis, Matt Murray, Rick Neal, Danile Nelson, Dean Nicolson, Sean Nittner, Laura Norton, Candi & Chris Norwood, Bryan Nothem, Mike Nudd, Duane O'Brien, Nick O'Connell, Esteban Osorio, Ray Otus, Vivian Paul, Cameron H. Peck, Patrick Pelham, Antoine Pempie, Ariel Pereira, Stuntlau Pérez, brian peters, Rusty Phillips, Markus Plötz, Misha Polonsky, Christopher Porter, Daryl Putman, Linus Råde, Martin Ralya, Kaelon Reddish, David Reed, Josh Rensch, Clyde Rhoer, D. Richards, Mark & Colleen Riley, James Ritter, Elise Roberts, Daniel & Trista Robichaud, Frank Rohrer, James Romanchuk, Lilith & Alexander Rose, Erica Schmitt, Mike Sergio, Michael Setteducati, Charley Sharp, Rachelle Shelkey, Shervyn, Ellen Siergiej, Alex Silverstein, Ramanan Sivaranjan, Patrick Sloan, Sean Smith, Harvey Smith, Bob Smith, Kevin Sonney, Seth Spurlock, Eric Stewart, Jimmie Stewart, Tayler Stokes, Christopher Stone-Bush, Alexander Stone-Tharp, Travis Stout, Jeremy Strandberg, Andrew Suarez, Matthew Sullivan-Barrett, Adam Surber, Matthew Swetnam, Josh Symonds, Therese Szymanski, Tapia & Soto, Thomas Tarlton, Gary Thompson, Angie Thum, Erik Tietyen, Rachel Tougas, Aaron Tranes, Peter Troia, Twitchytail, Colin Urbina, James R. Vance, Trenton Vartabedian, Kyle Ver Steeg, Tom Vlietstra, Zhan W., Kristy Wagner, Alisha Walton, Simon Ward, Joe Wasson, Christopher Weeks, Donald Welsh, Gavin White, Will, Brian Williams, Kevin Wine, Bennett Winter, Porter Wiseman, Andrew Yeckel, Casey Young, and Judah Zakoor

Thumpers

Peter Adkison, Donna Almendrala, Callum Artso, Phillip Bailey, Paul Beakley, John Beynon, Nathan Black, Barak Blackburn, Alex Blue, Eden Brandeis, André Brynkus, Tim Card, Michelle Carlson, DJ CherryPie, Richard Churchill, Brendan Conway, Raechel Coon, Brian M. Creswick, Samwise Crider, Paul & Sabrina Croucher, Michael Crowley, Andrew Dacey, Mikael Dahl, Henry Dannyson, Dominic DeCesare, Rym DeCoster, Vivian Dillon, Taylor Eichen, Michael Emrick, Julio Escajedo, Charles Etheridge-Nunn, Colin Fahrion, Dave Farabee, Colin Ferrie, Evan Flance Flance, Jasmine Friedrich,

Prudence Gaelor, Alex Gagnon, John Gamble, Antero Garcia, paul geer, Shanna Germain, Nick Golding, Daniel Gougian, Damon Griffin, Eric Groo, Jean-Philippe Guérard, Leah Gustavson, Christine Hamilton, Phil Hanley, Clarine Harp, Amanda Hawes, Michael Hill, Steve Holder, Simon Inglis, J2, Steve Jakoubovitch, Patrick Jedamzik, Scott Jenks, Harry Johansson, Judd Karlman, J T Keogh, Kate Kirby, John Kohn III, Jonathan Korman, Kraken, Kathryn Kramer, Michael Krauss, Jennifer Kyrnin, Taylor LaBresh, Sophie Lagace, Michael Langford, Jérôme Larré, Larry, Weena Legault, Samantha Lobello, Larry Lynch-Freshner, Katharine Magill, Kevin J. Maroney, C. W. Marshall, Jeff Mays, Josh McGraw, Paul McLean, Sarah Meyer, Mark Miller, Thomas Miller, Michael Moore, Kelly Moore, Richard Moran, David Moskowitz, Adrienne Mueller, Samuel Munilla, Larry Nehring, Brian Newman, Claus Nielsen, John Nienart, Guillaume Nocker, Keri Oleniach, Angela Oliver, Dan Panamaroff, Tom 'palfrey' Parker, Lemmo Pew, Benjamin Pharr, Mei Pollack, Jonathan Quigley, Kirk Rahusen, Hunter Rauscher, Matthew Recenello, Thomas Rim, John Roberts, Noam Rosen, Matthew Ross, Richard Ruane, Richard Ryan, Justin Schmid, Carl Schnurr, Matthew Seagle, Brandon Shalansky, Daniel Sheron, Matt Shoemaker, Steve Sick, Les and Dashiell Simpson, Julie Southworth, Ashley Speed, Xavier Spinat, Stephen Sproul, Daniel Stack, John Stavropoulos, Michael Stevens, Rachael Storey, Justin T, Brennan Taylor, Jeremy Tidwell, Anna Toone, Chris Truebe, Beth Tsai, Moyra Turkington, Erik Tylkowski, Nicola Urbinati, Kelley Vanda, Peetu Virkkala, Kaisa Vitikainen, Arthur Von Eschen, Rachel E. S. Walton, Evan Wargon, Beckett Warren, Rachel and Matt Watersong, Steven Watkins, Nicolaas Webb, William Weiler, Amy White, Michael Wight, Andrew Williams, Chris Williams, Stephanie Wilson, Marcia Worley, Victor Wyatt, Ming Yang, Tobiah Zarlez, and Sam Zeitlin

Runners

Kim Aar, Rob Abrazado, John Anderson, Joe Aponick, Paul Baldowski, Dave Bapst, Tracy Barnett, Meera Barry, Tim Batiuk, Stephen Beck Fey, Dan Behlings, Caitie Belle, Scott

Bennett, Andreas Bertossi, blackcoat, Jason Blalock, Matt & Nykki Boersma, Igor "Bone," Emily Care Boss, Jeb Boyt, Thomas Bybjerg Brock, Kelly Brown, Christopher Bryan, James Burzelic, Rob Bush, Alex C.-Trépanier, Gerald Cameron, Kate Candelaria, Travis Casey, Emily Catedral, Pedro Cendejas II, Brendan Clougherty, Dave Coe, Robert Corr, Rabbit Lord Cottonthumps, Ross Cowman, Michael Cox, Basil Craig, Brad Crosslin, Matias Dahlbäck, Stentor Danielson, Jonathan Davis, Elizabeth Dell, Zane Dempsey, Clinton Dreisbach, Scot Drew, Bryant Durrell, Henning Elfwering, Timothy Elrod, Bradley Eng-Kohn, Dexter Family, Paul-Thomas Ferguson, Ken Finlayson, Denise Foreman, Lowell Francis, Brian Franzman, Allen Fritts, Jeremiah Frye, Miles Gaborit, Travis Geery, Wiliam Gerke, Pedro Gil, Roger Giner-Sorolla, Michael Godesky, Golsteadski Family, Derek Gour, Ephraim Gregor, Jonathan Griffith, Matt Gwinn, Christopher Haffner, Cat Hariton, John Harper, Drew Harpunea, Victoria Hawthorne, Morgan Hay, Elliot Hayward, Albert Hernandez, Josh Hiebert, Caroline Hobbs, Andrew Hopwood, Jim Hughes, Jordan Hunt, Neal Hyde, imachuchu, Sara Jaffer, Johan Jaurin, Sam Jones, Emma Jones, Gary Kacmarcik, Isaac Karth, John Kennedy, Andrew Kenrick, Rene Kerkdyk, Louis Klay, Greg Klein, Jonathan Klick, Róbert Kovács, Klaus Ole Kristiansen, Dana Kubilus, Patrick Lacz, Sam LaFleche, John Lammers, Harry Lee, Nick Leiby, Jonah Lemkins, Harry Lewis, Phil Lewis, Mousekins Lewis, Michael Llaneza, Daniel Lofton, Alexandra Logan, Alexis Long, Michele Lord, Erika Lozano, Aldona M, Mark & Marissa (Magpie Games), Max Mahaffa, Jeremy Mahr, Steve Mains, Jamie Manley, Marcy, Anna Maurya, Ralph Mazza, Alec McEachern, Philip McElmurray, Matthew McFarland, Jake McGrath, Josh McIllwain, Tim McPherson, Rachel McWhirter, Kieren Medley, Hans Messersmith, Edmund Metheny, Emanuel James Miller, Justin Miller, Aaron MIller, Kristopher J Miller, Kyle Milner, Nathan Mitchell, Matthew Molumby, John Moran, Randy Mosiondz, James Mullins, Drew Nall, Matthew Nielsen, Andrew Nienaber, Mike Olson, Justus Pang, Matt Parker, Joel Pearce, Megan Pedersen, Frederick Pennington IV, Kevin "Chroma" Petker, Ben Pippin, Tun Kai Poh, Max & Kate Porter, Brendan Power, Michael Pureka, Andrew Quinn, Mike Quintanilla, Aaron

Rahlfs, Joshua Ramsey, Dave Rezak, Mark Richardson, Leonard Richardson, Alex Roberts, Jesse Roberts, Craig Robertson, Piper Robertson, Richard Rogers, Sarahtops Rogers, Vasishta Roske, Eva S, Elsa S. Henry, Roy Sachleben, Daniel Salcido, Sammo, Joe Schelin, Daniel Schlegel, Aniket Schneider, Oliver Scholes, J. Schultz, Daniel Sellers, Allegra Selzer, Guy Shalev, Jane Sheard, Victoria Short, Paul Showalter, Michael Siebold, Rustin Simons, Anders Smith, Kristina Smithman, Andy Spore, Guy Srinivasan, Steven Stimach, Bryant Stone, Storium.com, Mike Sugarbaker, Veles Svitlychny, Tom Switzenberg, Jay Sylvano, Marek Szkaradek, Etienne T. Harvey, William Talbott, Chris Thompson, Joel Thurston, Christopher Trdan, Faith U., Carrie Ulrich, Jeroen Van Lier, Anne Vinkel, waelcyrge, Drew Walker, Jonathan Walton, Marley Warren, Kadeem Warren, Witek Wasilewski, John Welsby, Wesrolter, Kerry White, Khrystian Wildes, Ian Williams, Sara Williamson, Sean Michael Winslow, Jason and Kai Wodicka, Rich Woods, wraith808, and Yanni

Diggers

Seth Abel, Stras "Hopper" Acimovic, ack ack ack ack, Rishi Agrawal, Allan, Svend Andersen, Mikael Andersson, APGamingREAL, Vincent Arebalo, Michael Atlin, Misha B, Matt Ballert, Erik Banner, Don Barnes, James Barratt, Alan Bartholet, Jonas Becker-Tietz, Torben Bellinghoff, Kevin Bender, Brainstormer Bester, Marco Bignami, John Bogart, Oliver Bollmann, Kurt Boucher, John Boyle, Simon Brake, Jon Bristow, Shane Brogan, Benjamin Brown, Joshua Brumley, Stephanie Bryant, Bubu Rabbit and Darky Rabbit, John Bunny, Kenneth Burgener, Anthony Butcher, Alicia Butteriss, Pedro Pablo Calvo, Suzene Campos del Toro, Hari Capra, Milo Careaga, Andi Carrison, Mindy Chua (:, Krzysztof Chyla, Frank Clark, Ewen Cluney, Russell Collins, Fractured Comics, Matthew Cooper, Joseph Cortese, Brianna And Corwyn, Dylan Craine, Giulia Cursi, Craig Curtis, Fernando D., Jeremy Daly, Alex Davis, Ryohei Deguchi, Jim DelRosso, Thomas Delrue, Thomas Demkey, Daniele Di Rubbo, Francis Dickinson, James Dillane, Curly Dimmick, Rob Donoghue, Bastian Dornauf, Evan Doyle, James Dunbier, Harlan DuPree, Bryce Duzan, Jayle Enn,

Aleksandr Ermakov, Katherine Fackrell, Kevin Farnworth, Jarrod Farquhar-Nicol, Declan Feeney, Carrie-Anne Ferrie, AJ Fieldhouse, Adam Flynn, Jay Fong, Josh Fox, Adam Fox, Melissa Frank, Loren Frerichs, Dave Friederich, Fiery Gatoh, David Geisler, Pip Gengenbach, Simon Gerrard, Hel Gibbons, Felix Girke, Ian Glodich, Angry Goblin, Beverley Gordon, Alex Gray, Megan Greathouse, Tomer Gurantz, Gwathdring, Dan Hallock, Will Hancock, Michael Harrel, Seth Harris, Ace W. Hart, Christian Häusler, Kevin Heckman, Patrice Hédé, Tommy Heinig, Steve Hickey, Andrew Hill, Henrik Høeg, Cody Holden, James Holdridge, Amy Hood, Jeffrey Hosmer, Wei-Hua Hsieh, Jared Hunt, Marcus Ilgner, Chris Jean, S J Jennings, Jester, Daniel Jiménez, Dan Curtis Johnson, Erik Johnson, Kelly Jolliffe, Doug Jones, Matthew Kabik, Ben Kaser, Cory Katz, Jeremy Kear, Jussi Kenkkilä, Michael Kennedy, Christopher Kettle-Frisby, Michael "Owlbear Cowboy" Kidd, Aidan Macallister Kimber, Motoi Kito, David Klein, Adam Koebel, Chris Krueger, Kat L., Ted Lai, Mercedes Lamb, Andrew Larimer, Connor Lemp, Eric Levanduski, Michael Lingefelt, Steve Lord, Fred Lott, David M., Springstep Macarthaigh, Keith Mageau, Frank J. Manna, Ryan Mannix, David Margowsky, Mark, Trevis Martin, Łukasz Matysiak, Justin Mazz, Donogh McCarthy, M McGranaghan, William McMahan, Andy Meadows, Warren Merrifield, Alisson Vitório Mestre das Antigas, Johnstone Metzger, Matthew Miller, James Miller, Daniel Miller, Adam Minnie, Deryl Mitzen, David Morrison, Jim Morrison, Alistair Morrison, Sascha Müller, Lukas Myhan, Eric Nieudan, Morten Njaa, Robert Nolan, Dan Noland, Anders Nordberg, Ted Novy, Tim Noyce, Michael Nutter, Emmett O'Brien-Wheeler, Phoenix Osiris, Nadja Otikor, Sean Owen, Lenny Pacelli, William Palmer, Spencer Pasero, Reverance Pavane, Ryan Perrin, Nicholas Peterson, Ric Philbin, Tom Pleasant, John Poe, Saverio Porcari, John Potts, Derek Pounds, Bill Powell, Jeff Prather, Adam Rajski, Ian Raymond, Scott Reichelt, Gerrit Reininghaus, Bryan Rennekamp, Michael Richards, Jordan Richer, Paul & Shannon Riddle, Matti Rintala, Steven Robert, Xavier Robledo, Joel Rojas, Ben Rosenbaum, Sebastian Ross, Andreas Rugård Klæsøe, David Rymer, Eduard Saller, Jane Samborski, Timothy "Samwise7" Harper, Dub Saunders, schizoid from rpggeek, Will Scilacci, Hannah Shaffer, Aaron Shapiro,

Marcus Shepherd, Gail Sherman, Kim Shier, Kyle Simons, Tim Sims, Andrew Sinsbury, Jeffrey N Smith, Adrian Smith, Trip Space-Parasite, Aaron Stanger, Starlight, Keith Stetson, Manny Suarez, Matteo Suppo, Dan Suptic, Rob T, Twitch The Terrible, Stephen Thomson, Tapani Tiilikainen, Dylan Tobias, Jason Tocci, Federico (Dimofamo) Totti, Matthew Tyler-Jones, Kendall Uyeji, Alex Valiushko, Allen Varney, Phil Vecchione, Markus Viklund, Christopher Vollick, Aarre Vuorio, Tom Walker, Kevin Walker, Mark Wallace, Noel Warford, Andrew Watkins, Darren Watts, WC Pemm, Benjamin Welke, Matt Wetherbee, Jeremy Wheat, Jamie Wheeler, Adam White, Jim "T.W.Wombat" White, Barac Wiley, Mook Wilson, Avonelle Wing, Brandon Wolff, Rohan Wolsey, J Brad Woodfin, Diane Worden, Sam Wright, Yungen Wu, Joshua Young, Jason Youngdale, Valerio Zanghi, Stefan "Zant" Riewe, Z.L. Zhou, Jin Zhu, Ryan Ziegler, and Thomas Zimolo

Retailers and Distributors

Jason Pitre (CA), Games and Stuff (US), and Graham Walmsley (UK)

Index

N

Names 31, 80, 86
Non-player Character 16
NPC 16, 60, 61, 112

O

Ongoing 23

P

Panic 29, 33, 35, 36, 40, 43, 58, 112
Panicking 43
Pay Attention 34, 95, 96
PC 16, 112, 113
Pikas 99
Playbook 16, 27
Player Character 16, 25, 27, 35, 113
Player Moves 21, 22, 33
Playsets 16, 60, 79
Predator Moves 24, 64
Predators 49, 59, 60, 64, 65, 84, 90, 102, 103, 104
Principles 51

R

Relax 36
Resist Panic 33, 43
Retire 42, 47
Retirement 46, 113